VENTURING
WHERE FEW HAVE
DARED TO GO

Standing on the DMZ(Demilitarized Zone
dividing North and South Korea)
with South Korea soldiers, 1968

Gene Burgess

Venturing Where Few Have Dared To Go

iUniverse books may be ordered through booksellers or by contacting:

iUniverse
1663 Liberty Drive
Bloomington, IN 47403
www.iuniverse.com
844-349-9409

Because of the dynamic nature of the Internet, any web addresses or links contained in this book may have changed since publication and may no longer be valid. The views expressed in this work are solely those of the author and do not necessarily reflect the views of the publisher, and the publisher hereby disclaims any responsibility for them.

Any people depicted in stock imagery provided by Getty Images are models, and such images are being used for illustrative purposes only. Certain stock imagery © Getty Images.

Scripture quotations marked NIV are taken from the Holy Bible, New International Version®. NIV®. Copyright © 1973, 1978, 1984 by International Bible Society. Used by permission of Zondervan. All rights reserved. [Biblica]

ISBN: 978-1-6632-3648-7 (sc)
ISBN: 978-1-6632-3715-6 (e)

Library of Congress Control Number: 2022904592

Print information available on the last page.

iUniverse rev. date: 06/06/2022

Contents

Comments By Friends

Gene Burgess has encountered enough drama and adventure in his world-wide ministry to fill several books, so sequels may be in order. Here in Memphis, however, he is known for his special ability to connect with people from all walks of life, a talent that has endeared him to inner-city pastors, civic leaders and law-enforcement officials alike. I am proud to call this dedicated tireless pastor and humanitarian my friend.

District Attorney General Amy Weirich

Gene Burgess has definitely lived a life on the edge. He could have settled into a successful career as a pharmacist, but answered the call of God to full-time ministry and has never looked back. His adventures have involved world-wide evangelism, servicemen's missions, and pastoral ministry. Gene Burgess has been inducted into the Hall of Champions of Tennessee District Assemblies of God. He is a man worthy of double honor!

Terry G. Bailey
Superintendent of Tennessee District Assemblies of God

I met Pastor Gene Burgess Easter Sunday 2001. I had been a Christian for about 2 years and was in recovery for addiction to Methamphetamine.

I had been a member of Bartlett First Assembly for about 18 months when Pastor Burgess and his associate pastor began a ministry school called Mid-South Master's Commission. Pastor Burgess helped me transition from recovering addict to minister of the gospel in those two years. Pastor Burgess made sure that each student of MSMC got the opportunity to do all aspects of ministry.

At twenty-three years old and no experience outside internships, I served as Student Pastor, Associate Pastor, and Transition Pastor under Pastor Gene Burgess' leadership over the following 9 years. I was his final Staff Pastor in what he has said was "the most fun years of his 50 years of ministry." We ministered together to kids all over the inner city of Memphis, we built a brand new Family Life Center, celebrated many victories, and cried many tears.

In August of 2013, we began to discuss transition to his retirement. I let him know I would stay on until his replacement was found and he said, "Johnny, the new leadership is you." He spent the next 18 months preparing the church to go from an experienced, seasoned, traditional minister to a young, passionate, inexperienced, unorthodox pastor.

I could have spent this page telling you of all the people who were saved, baptized, or the problems that I watched Pastor solve masterfully, but the thing that has impacted my ministry and life the most is the fact that he believed in me more than I did, trusted me with more than I thought I could handle, and truly lived out loud the mantra that "there is no success without a successor."

Pastor Johnny Byrd, Senior Pastor
Bartlett First Assembly of God, now called "Legacy Church of Bartlett"

1

Adventures in Far North Canada and Alaska

As a kid, I could hardly wait for Saturday mornings to come! This was the day that Sergeant Preston of the **Royal Canadian Mounted Police** was featured on the radio. Something exciting was always happening in the far north. I would wait breathlessly to hear Sergeant Preston of the RCMP come on the air with the spine-tingling words, "Mush you huskies! Onward!" It never seemed to matter how cold it was or how ruthless the "bad guys" were, Sergeant Preston and his dog team never failed to catch the outlaws. Those were the days before TV, but the narrators could almost make the listeners see the blazing red uniforms of the RCMP as their adventures unfolded.

One of my dreams growing up was to see these famous Red Coats patrolling the frozen Canadian north – or to see dog sleds racing across the Alaskan frozen tundra. Many years later, Heather and I engaged in full-time evangelism in many countries, including Canada and the northern reaches of Alaska. Can you imagine, one of the very first things we saw when we crossed the border from the U.S. into Canada was a red-coated Mountie astride a horse? It was then I remembered those earlier years, getting up on Saturday mornings and listening to Sergeant Preston bravely enforcing the laws of our northern neighbor.

One of the most fascinating things that I remember about the Sergeant and the Mounties was their dog sleds. Not only did they have their own dogs and sleds, they had dog sled races over several hundred miles of frozen tundra. The "Iditarod" was the name of this annual event. Most of the dogs were huskies, a type of German Shepherd, with heavy coats able to withstand the piercing cold as they raced across vast stretches of snow. If you ever visit these areas, do not waste time looking for roads, for there are none.

It mystified me how these races could take place across unmarked routes that ran several hundred miles. The dogs and their owners would stop at night and rest in the white wilderness. The next day they would continue as the sun rose. It had to be a grueling experience. One thing for sure, the prizes for winners were minimal compared to the risk and energy expended by those who invested huge amounts of time and money for the honor of winning. Year after year they participate in these races, competing to win the coveted trophy. Many critics of these races claim the sled drivers are cruel to the dogs, or that the dogs are abused. However, nothing could be further from the truth. The dogs are excited every time they go on a race or a hunt. Racing seems to be part of their DNA. Certainly, they are rarely treated cruelly.

I must investigate how the dog sleds keep from getting lost in the vast unmarked snowy wilderness. Also, I am not sure exactly how many dogs run with each sled and how long these races last. So, hang on and we will soon find the answers to these questions.

HEADING TO SEATTLE AND FAIRBANKS, ALASKA

In 1969 we were delighted with an invitation to conduct meetings in Alaska. The first of many exciting adventures for us began with the long road trip from our home in Memphis 2,200 miles north to **Seattle.**

Heather was excited that she might entertain real Eskimo children with puppets and Bible stories. I was excited that we would be travelling to a land of snow and dog sleds, sharing the Gospel with people we had only dreamed of meeting.

We planned to travel by car to Seattle on the West Coast and then north by plane to Alaska with our 3-month-old daughter, Deborah. As you might expect, the further north from Memphis we drove, the colder it got. Early March winds whipped at the snow that had been plowed into white banks beside the interstate. In spite of the heavy equipment in our trunk, our car became harder to control. I finally pulled off the highway at a gas station a few miles from Seattle and told the owner that our car was beginning to fishtail. The manager asked, "Have you checked under your car lately?"

I was not sure what he was talking about, but when I found a flashlight and looked, I saw huge clumps of ice and snow clinging to the underside of our vehicle. The gentleman explained, "All you need is a hammer and you can knock most of that loose."

The problem was, I could hit a gas line or knock a hole in the exhaust system if I was not careful. I was quickly learning about travelling in winter in the Northwestern States.

We had arranged to stop in Seattle for a church youth conference. Toward evening as we continued north the snow got deeper. The snowplows had cleared a passage through it on one lane of the highway, leaving snow stacked up on either side of the interstate. When we topped the last mountain, we looked down onto a valley. Spread out before us was the vast city Seattle. The sun was just setting and the city began coming alive with thousands of tiny streetlights winking on in the twilight.

I stopped and called the pastor from a phone booth to check on arrangements related to the conference scheduled there. (No cell phones back in those days.) The pastor in Seattle seemed nervous and upset about something. "Can you come meet me in the church office as soon as possible?" he asked.

The request was unusual this late in the evening. However, I followed the directions to the address he gave me. When we arrived, the first thing the pastor blurted out was, "**Our Youth Pastor has just been murdered**!"

I stood there dumbfounded. Apparently, the youth pastor had been working as a cashier in a convenience store when two men had burst in and shot him.

The news had spread like wildfire. The church members were in shock and the young people were numb with grief. As for us, I wondered how this would affect our arrangements. We had planned several evenings of meetings for the church, with a strong youth emphasis.

The church had to make several immediate decisions. There was a funeral to plan. What about our meetings – should they be cancelled? The pastor decided we should go ahead with the meetings as planned. Arrangements were quickly put in place for the funeral and the local high school excused students who wanted to attend. Almost the entire student body came to the funeral. Many of the teens who attended were touched both emotionally and spiritually by the event. In some ways, many of those young people being so deeply impacted by the death of their leader, were brought face to face with the brevity of life and the necessity of preparing for eternity. The meetings continued as scheduled, giving people a chance to come together to face their grief and pray with each other. In that sense, the timing of our visit with the church was ideal.

After those meetings, we left our car at the Seattle airport and flew north to Anchorage, Alaska.

ALASKA

For most people, Alaska is a mystery. Some used to call it "Seward's Ice Box." In 1867 the U.S. had purchased the territory from Russia for $7 million, which amounted to roughly 2 cents per acre. Alaska achieved statehood in 1959.

It was not very long until the purchase of Alaska proved to have been a lucrative investment. Millions of dollars of oil and gas reserves were discovered there, plus the logging and fishing industries that quickly developed brought in more millions of dollars. In time, Alaska became a tourist destination. Texans like to brag that theirs is the largest state in the Union, but actually Alaska is the largest.

The most popular annual event in the far north is dog sled racing. The Iditarod Races draw hundreds of people annually. As promised, I found that these races cover 1,000 miles and require about 9 days to complete. The competition involves sleds, each pulled by 16 dogs, and driven by the captain called the "musher."

They race through the snow across hundreds of miles of uncharted territory – territory that holds many hidden dangers. In the past, the prize has consisted of a Dodge Pick-Up truck, plus cash and the honor of winning. Considering the expense and danger of the race, that prize is small.

MINISTERING IN THE LAND OF THE MIDNIGHT SUN

Our first meetings were scheduled in Anchorage, followed by Fairbanks, and then Barrow, all the way north beyond the Arctic Circle. Both Fairbanks and Anchorage are modest sized cities, but the flight to Barrow takes one to a whole different world. On those March days spent in Barrow, the sunlight never totally left the horizon. For four or five hours each night the sun dimmed to a deep blue before returning to its brilliant yellow glory. Blackout curtains made rooms dark enough for sleeping.

The flight on the jet passenger plane from Fairbanks to Barrow required a few hours. Most of the passengers we travelled with were involved in the oil industry in Barrow and the coastal oil fields there. Normally, in those days men wore suits and ties when travelling by air. These men's attire consisted of grubby work clothes. Many of them on the flight brought along various tools and equipment.

As the plane neared our destination in Barrow, all we could see through the windows were ice and snow. As we touched down, we definitely wondered – Where are we? Barrow, being above the Arctic Circle, looks to be part of another planet! We landed in a "white-out" – the wind blowing the snow into the air so ferociously that visibility was nearly zero. We could not see the runway nor even the ground. The pilot landed with amazing expertise and reversed the engines, easing us to a stop. The brakes alone would not have stopped the plane on the icy runway.

We carefully wrapped our 3-month-old baby in blankets, gathered up our bags and stepped out into a silent world of white. The one small structure barely visible ahead turned out to be the air terminal. Standing around it was a small group of ruddy-faced men clad in fur-lined parkas. And then – we saw the pastor who had come to greet us. Thank the Lord!

The church in Barrow was most unusual in that the temperature remained set at 50 degrees inside during the services. I was told I must dress "appropriately" as befits the dignity of a minister. I spoke, while shivering in the heaviest suit I had packed. The congregation was predominantly Eskimo, dressed in heavy beautiful fox and seal skin coats.

We had brought along our projector and sound equipment. That first night we showed the people videos of our journeys elsewhere in the world. We had hoped the presentation would draw the villagers to the meetings. At the end of our first service, the pastor said, "It's a waste to show these people other countries. Most of our people have never even seen green grass."

I requested we try again a second night to see if people came back, drawn by the video presentation. He was amazed that even more attended the following night. There had been very little Gospel preached in this region and these folks were responsive to the message of salvation. It was a rewarding place to preach!

The facial features of the Eskimos we met appeared Asian – rather like Mongolians. I looked for igloos in the village, and found not a single one. These folks lived in simple wooden homes, and would only construct igloos as temporary shelters when they went on extended hunting or fishing trips. The pastor gave Heather and me a little update on what to expect in this town. He said, "Tomorrow a liquor flight will arrive." Postal regulations prohibited sending alcohol through the mail, so the liquor would be sent by plane, parcel post. The pastor said, "Tomorrow when the flight arrives, you'll see little children leading grown men, stone drunk, falling into the snow drifts." Unfortunately, he was right. The next day there were drunk men lying in the snow drifts right in front of the church.

During our stay, the pastor gave us a brief tour of the region on his snowmobile. Our little baby, Deborah, rode on Heather's back Eskimo style under her borrowed parka as we glided over the frozen Arctic landscape. We swirled through the drifts and did wheelies, unhindered by speed limits! What a ride!

One extremely interesting event we experienced on this trip was visiting the home of a church member who had recently shot a polar bear. The hide and meat are major sources of income for this region. We were invited into the front room of a small wooden house where an Eskimo man was cleaning the polar bear hide. It was stretched out across the living room floor and secured fur-side-down. He was scraping the inside of the skin so that no fat or meat remained. Incidentally, his young son was eating a can of Ravioli for breakfast, which I found amusing. Of course, people enjoy the meat of the polar bear as well as the meat of the seals. However, the real prizes are the hides of the animals that make their way to the wholesalers in the "Lower 48."

2

Hazardous Travel Through
Western Canada

Darkness had closed in around us quickly that night in Canada, as we navigated the narrow road through the snow, headed for Regina, Saskatchewan. Our way was lit solely by the shivering stars in the winter sky and by the headlights of 2 cars: ours, and the car we were following, until the car ahead suddenly slammed on his brakes and skidded to a stop, blocking our path. The driver jumped out and ran toward us waving a rifle. I froze in terror, not able to believe what was happening.

The driver of that car was a stranger we had met at the last gas station where we had stopped. This fellow customer had begun chatting with us. When he heard we were going to Regina he seemed delighted and told us that was his home. "You can follow me if you like. I know a shortcut," he offered. Since it was very late and we had a 70-mile drive ahead, his offer of leading us on a shortcut had seemed like a God-send.

Soon we were on our way. We followed our new friend deep into a snowy wilderness. The only problem was, we had not the faintest idea where we were going. He was leading us on a little road that was not identified on our map. And then, about 20 minutes into the trip, it happened! Our new "friend" was suddenly blocking our path on the narrow road with snow stacked up on both sides, trapping us.

His interior light flashed on as the stranger opened his door and we'd caught a glimpse of him grabbing a rifle from the back seat. He ran to the driver's window of our car waving the gun. Who was this guy we had trusted to lead us? Stories of thrill killers who for no reason shot people on lonely highways, flashed through my mind. Was this how our lives would end? We had no idea where we were nor how to get to the main highway for help. What was he going to do to us?

He cursed in excitement and yelled, "Did you see that?"

I cautiously cracked the window and shouted, "See what?"

"That deer! Didn't you see it?" He stomped around wildly in the snow, peering into the darkness and cursing excitedly. "Hey, tell you what, you guys keep following this road. You're almost to the main highway ahead. Ten minutes. You'll be OK. I'm gonna follow this deer," he hollered as he took off into a field following deer tracks. We managed to ease around his car and continue our journey.

That incident was only one of many fearsome events we experienced on the highways of Canada, our neighbor to the north.

The questions is, what was I - a Southern boy born and raised in Memphis - doing driving through the snowdrifts of Canada in the middle of winter? Well, after graduating from pharmacy school, I felt God was re-directing me from selling medicine to preaching the Gospel. People like me were called evangelists, and we traveled from church to church preaching nightly "revival" services, encouraging people to live for God, and encouraging them to greater faith in His love and power in their lives.

I, along with my wife Heather, had followed what we felt was God's calling here in the States, and also overseas. In doing so, we had flown on poorly maintained third world airlines in typhoon season, ridden in the open ocean in a tiny outrigger boat, and faced other perils. But we never dreamed of the hazards of traveling westward on the Canadian highways in subfreezing temperatures and severe blizzard conditions. The Trans-Canada Highway covers almost 5.000 miles, starting at the eastern seaboard and ending at the Pacific coast of British Columbia. There were days when we traveled from city to city not really certain that we would make it safely to the next preaching engagement. I can say with confidence that my prayer life was greatly strengthened.

Even looking at a map we had no idea exactly how far it was from city to city. Sometimes we felt that those who organized our trip did not have the faintest idea either. One thing for sure, we saw lots and lots of snow. Over the grain fields of the prairies, stocks of winter wheat barely poked their heads over the top of the snow drifts, and even some telephone poles were almost obliterated.

That first time we headed for the Canadian northland, our final stop in the USA was Minneapolis. That city has a reputation for being extremely cold in the winter - and it was! The distance from **Minneapolis** to **Winnipeg** is about 500 miles. Our trip involved driving on two-lane highways, which made me nervous because there was no median. As we continued on north, it seemed that the car did not handle quite right. I pulled over at one point and got out to check on the problem. When I stepped out of the car the highway was so slick that I fell flat on my back. Fortunately, it didn't hurt. We soon discovered that as long as you are driving on a straight course on ice and hard-packed snow - which we were - and did not slam on your brakes, you could drive fairly safely at 70 miles an hour. Yet, stopping could be another problem.

AN ELECTRIFIED CAR

One night during that trip, the temperature plummeted well below zero, and the next morning our car doors were frozen solid. I went around to the trunk, but it was frozen shut completely. I asked somebody in the apartment where we were staying why I was having so much trouble with my car. He suggested we get a can of de-icer. We sprayed de-icer around the edges of the trunk, which magically allowed the lid to open easily. Now the challenge was to get the four doors open, which were frozen tightly too. I could not even get my key into the lock. Again, the neighbor explained I just had to spray de-icer into every place I would put my key, and like magic all the doors and the trunk opened easily.

Then he asked a question, "Did you also forget to plug in your car?" I had been teased by Canadians about so many things, I thought this was one more joke. He explained, "Your gas line is totally frozen and your engine is frozen. So, you need a block heater."

Again, this was one time I thought someone was going to get a laugh at my expense. But he pointed down the street and said, "There's a small auto shop where they can put a block heater in your car for you. It will keep the oil from freezing and give the engine just a little heat."

Once again, he asked, "Did you notice those little electrical fittings on the sides of buildings? Also, we have electric connections on the parking meters." He continued, "Your engine can freeze solid in 15 minutes, so the mechanic will also run an electrical cord from the motor through the grill on your car and you can simply plug it into one of those outlets. I felt foolish but noticed everyone was plugging in their cars, and it worked very well. Thus, for the remainder of our six months on the Canadian prairies I didn't forget to plug in my car every night.

A HAIR-RAISING EVENT WITH A GASOLINE TRUCK

The next challenge was to start the car, but I assumed this would be no problem since I had installed a brand new battery and block heater and had the engine checked thoroughly. To my surprise, when I turned on the ignition it made a little squeaking noise. And that was it. The neighbor shook his head and explained, "Since you have an automatic transmission in your car it won't start until you get it up to 35 miles an hour." But, how could I do this?

A truck driver who had been standing nearby sauntered over, pulled off his cap and scratched his head, observing the situation. Finally, he made a suggestion. He was willing, he said, to help me, although his plan was *extremely dangerous*. But he assured me it was the only way to get my car started in zero-degree weather. He offered to attach my car to the bumper of his gasoline truck, and when he got his huge tanker up to 35 miles an hour, he would signal me and I would be able to start my car.

Again, I thought he was joking. However, if he *wasn't* joking, my concern with the plan was, his chain was no longer than 12 feet. So, if my car started according to his idea, it appeared I would have only 12 feet to stop before running into the back of his truck. Anyhow, there were no more choices, so feeling like a real-life Dumbo, I let him chain my car to the rear bumper of his huge silver gasoline tanker. He started very slowly and gradually we reached 35 miles an hour. He gave me the signal and I turned the key. Sure enough, our car started! This was like living in a whole new world! After stopping and unhooking the chain, the trucker tooted his horn and waved goodbye.

May I suggest that when you are having a boring day you chain your car to the back of a gasoline truck by a 12 foot chain! Exciting! Can you imagine how much fun I had when I got back to Memphis and every gasoline station attendant was bewildered to see this cord hanging out of my grill work. I jokingly explained to them that when I was in Canada mechanics electrified my car. Later, I would explain it was a special addition that kept my oil and engine from freezing.

We were very blessed that the Lord had opened the doors of some of the largest churches in Canada to receive us. One of the unique advantages to our style of meetings was that Heather conducted simultaneous activities for the children in a separate area. She used puppets and illustrated Bible stories with object lessons that included games, quizzes and prizes. The kids loved it, and the best part was, our meetings included the whole family.

Winnipeg Gospel Tabernacle in Winnipeg, Manitoba had a long history reaching back to the early days of Pentecost. It was one of the largest gospel churches in Canada, a thriving church pastored by Dr. Herb Barber. I was amazed at the excellent attendance night after night, even though it was snowing and temperatures dipped below zero. The pastor told us, "If the wind is not blowing the snow, people will come to the services. But," he urged us, "please don't come in the summer, for then the people will either be at the lake or in the fields."

My evangelist friends who all went to Florida in the winter thought I was crazy for heading into the frigid northlands. However, it worked out very well for us. *We had told the Lord we would go to the smallest church in the smallest town and not demand any certain amount of money if He would just open doors for us in larger churches that could cover our financial needs.*

Most of the churches we visited were small, so the members rarely saw a guest minister. They treated us with heart-warming enthusiasm and appreciation. I couldn't understand why more evangelists did not visit these places. These folks were eager to talk and visit with us at the conclusion of the services. A new voice, teaching the same truths as their own pastors, often expanded their understanding of the love and power of God as applied to their daily lives. We felt blessed to have been able to share in their lives, however briefly.

Of course, my other evangelist friends might assume that the offerings would be too small to meet their expenses. I had many evangelist friends who asked that a list of demands be met before scheduling special meetings in a church. Some asked to be put up in a comfortable motel and be given a food allowance rather than staying with local church members. Some asked the churches to cover travel expenses. Many pastors did not want to deal with the requests. We made no demands on the churches. Frankly, I did not watch the total offerings much. I knew they would be adequate.

Sometimes out west, we stayed in small farm homes that were barely visible from the highway because of the huge snow drifts. We stayed with one German family who were wonderful hosts. The first evening they had me park our car in their backyard. During the night, it snowed so heavily I could not even see our car the next morning! It was totally buried in snow, all except the silver radio arial protruding from a blanket of white. There was no way that we could have driven out of there on our own. The farmer assessed the situation, disappeared around a corner of the barn and soon returned leading a huge brown work horse. He seemed to know what he was doing, and attached a big chain underneath my car to the harness of his work horse. I could hardly believe my eyes! I watched this horse pull our heavy car out of the drifts to a nearby rural road. This couple was typical of countless lovely pioneering people we met in the Canadian prairies.

A MOST UNIQUE TELEPHONE

One day I asked one of the pastors we stayed with if I might use his telephone. He said, "Certainly, it's in the den." I walked into the den and looked for the telephone. My eyesight is not very good, but I did look everywhere and I could *not* find a telephone.

Somewhat embarrassed, I went back to the pastor and said, "I'm sorry, I can't find the phone." He asked me if I had looked on the wall. And on the wall, I *had* found an old-fashioned telephone - the style of phone that Andy Griffith used on his old TV comedy series. I told him that was the only thing I could find.

"That's it!" he assured me. I scratched my head. OK, I thought, all I have to do, I guess, is crank it two or three times and an operator will come on the line. I tried. Nothing happened. Now I was really embarrassed.

I asked the pastor if he could help me operate his phone. He cranked the phone a few more times and an operator came on the line just like on old TV programs. I tried not to laugh after learning an old-fashioned lesson.

Some of our meetings were planned by local Assemblies of God pastors. Others were planned by a strong international ministry called *Youth For Christ.* There was a day when this inter-faith ministry drew vast crowds of young people to weekly rallies in cities all across America and Canada. I worked with *Youth For Christ* in Memphis while I was in high school and later in college. At the Saturday night rallies there was always a contest between the

Memphis high schools to see which would have the best attendance – lots of cheering and excitement in those rallies. There were also contests for musical talent and Bible quiz teams. Those were great days!

A friend told us that *Youth For Christ* had planned a similar tour across Canada for the world-famous evangelist Billy Graham in his earlier years of ministry. His home was back in North Carolina, certainly not in Western Canada. Someone in their head office in Toronto had arranged for Mr. Graham a schedule that would take him from Ontario all the way to Alberta, (over 2,000 miles). Strangely, that is almost the same route that we would take years later. So, in essence we kept the same type schedule as Billy Graham - every night a different city, a different schoolhouse, or auditorium. He is reported to have exclaimed in exhaustion, "Even Jesus couldn't have kept up with a schedule like this one!"

I will relate two more stories full of high drama on the Canadian highways that winter.

THE MOUNTIES WERE MURDERED

After being pulled out of the snow drifts, we continued on our way. We looked for a place to get some hot coffee and a snack. There were few buildings of any kind and very limited traffic along that highway. We kept scanning the road ahead, but saw no place to pull into for a cup of coffee. Finally, we passed one little place that looked promising. When we saw nothing else on the horizon we stopped there for a quick snack before continuing on our way.

A short time later as we drove, I glanced over to a field on our right and saw a group of Mounties in their bright red uniforms with weapons drawn. I slowed as they headed their snowmobiles in our direction. Their grim faces made it obvious they were not on some kind of training mission. After all, this was in the middle of nowhere!

Again, my curious nature got the best of me and I wondered what Mounties were doing in the middle of nowhere, surrounded by a group of very ferocious barking dogs. I stopped and started to get out of the car to ask a few questions. About the time I stepped out of the car with my camera, the dogs lunged toward me and the Mounties began to holler, "Shut up and get back in the car!" I had no idea what was going on, but I could tell these policemen were not kidding.

We sat there for a few moments shaking, as these ferocious dogs continued barking and jumping around our car. There was no danger, but it was an unexpected and bewildering experience happening to us in this frozen wilderness. The lead sergeant came over to our car, still with his dogs in tow, and asked me if I knew what had happened back down the highway. Of course, I had no idea, but understood that he was very agitated and disturbed.

He explained how in a little restaurant a few miles back, a man had come in with guns blazing and shot two of their best Mounties in the back, and then quickly left. "Now we have every available policeman and Mountie in the region on the lookout. That's why our dogs are so agitated because of all the action." I did not need any more explanation. Quickly, we made our exit and continued on toward our destination. It dawned on us that we had just stopped at the very same restaurant at which the Mounties had been murdered, probably right after we left!

And one final story of our adventures on Canadian highways:

WHO WAS THE MAN WAVING A BLANKET?

Most people have never heard of Saskatoon, the second largest city in the province of Saskatchewan. It was the site of our next crusade, to be held in a large civic auditorium.

As I mentioned earlier, Canada's major east-west highway - the Trans Canada - runs basically just north of the border between the U.S. and Canada, all the way from the Atlantic to the Pacific. We travelled a good part of this highway when we left Winnipeg, Manitoba and travelled west to Saskatchewan and British Columbia. It was a very exciting time. So many lives touched by the power of God! We drove along the highway over 3,000 miles, never seeing the ground for almost six months.

On one particular stretch the road was clear and straight, so we probably were driving faster than we should have been. Out of the corner of my eye I thought I caught a glimpse of what looked like a figure ahead, holding a blanket. A man waving a blanket in the middle of nowhere? The weather was subfreezing and there were basically no houses in the area. We could not see any cars immediately ahead of us or behind us.

As a result of briefly spotting this strange sight, we gradually slowed down. As we topped a small rise, up ahead we saw a terrible accident. If we had not slowed down, we would have slammed into this fatal smash-up. A Greyhound bus had collided head-on with a cattle truck. It was not a pretty scene. Frankly, I did not want to take a close look.

The major question was, who or what was the figure waving the blanket on the side of the highway warning us that there was a terrible accident just ahead? There seemed to be no people living in the area, no cars, nothing! We began to ponder who this figure was. And the question that comes to mind so often looking back - was it an angel the Lord had sent to warn us of danger? We don't know. When we turned around and looked back to where the figure had been, he was gone. There was no passing vehicle that might have picked him up earlier. We are grateful to the Lord for His mercy once again.

We thank God for the protection He provided during those 6 months of travel on the winter roads of Canada. It was a priceless journey, and one we will never forget as we "ventured where few had dared to go."

3

Far From Home and Nowhere to Go

"Far from home and nowhere to go." What do you do when all your plans fall through, and it seems that God is a million miles away? When there appears to be no place to turn, and prayers seem to go unanswered? Here's what happened to us that winter in Canada.

We had spent 3 months in the frozen Canadian winter. But now it was time to head south. We had been blessed with many invitations to speak, mostly in California. We had been able to book meetings about six months in advance. We planned to travel down the west coast and end up speaking at conferences in Southern California, which appeared to be a great plan. Our final few winter months of travel would be in the southern USA with its pleasant temperatures.

There was only one problem: we had booked our meetings so far ahead that by December many of the pastors had changed their plans for one reason or another. One by one, for the 3 months we had planned to be on the southwest coast of USA, our meetings were cancelled or postponed for all but 2 weeks. This would mean driving all the way down the west coast from Canada to California for only 2 weeks. Then, we would have to make another trip of 2,000 miles back home to Memphis. This did not seem like a very logical plan.

As we sat in our car in a church parking lot in Edmonton, Alberta, we opened a letter that had just arrived. We had concluded some wonderful services in that flourishing church, but at this moment we were not feeling very elated. The letter informed us that those final 2 weeks in California had been cancelled. It dawned on us that almost every service for the next 3 months had to be rescheduled. This would be impossible without driving many thousands of extra miles. Thus, we sat in the parking lot bewildered and desperate for some direction.

We had adequate finances, but not enough for 3 months and not for a 2,000-mile trip across the USA at Christmas time when most churches were more interested in Santa Claus than conducting a revival meeting. There were some parts of the country where we were fairly well-known, but not way out here in western Canada. We were at a loss. Totally!

We sat in the parking lot in Edmonton praying, without a clue as to what to do, when out of nowhere Ken Bombay pulled his car up beside us and asked where we were going. Pastor Ken was one of the more outstanding pastors in western Canada. We had puzzled looks on our faces, because honestly, we did not have the faintest idea where we were going next.

SURPRISE CHRISTMAS IN CANADA

We told him our plans had changed, and we were unsure what to do. He asked, "Where are you going to spend Christmas?" We told him we had no idea. This generous pastor offered, "Why don't you come back to Calgary with us and spend the Christmas holidays in our home?" We were just blown away at such generosity. We have been amazed over the years at the miraculous way the Lord has intervened for us!

I dare anybody to talk about the "cold Canadians," accusing them of being unfriendly, because obviously this is not true for 99% of them. Accepting Pastor Ken's invitation, we turned around and drove south from Edmonton 200 miles back to Calgary to spend the holidays with Ken and Joan Bombay. We had a wonderful time visiting with these pastors of a thriving church in Calgary.

While we were with them, Ken suggested that since we had several more days off, we might like to go over and visit Banff. Banff is a world-famous national park in the Rocky Mountains of Canada, and is about 150 miles east of Calgary. The only warning he gave us, was to be sure and watch out for the mountain goats. They often stood in the middle of the highway and simply stared at the cars. If you hit one it would be a major offence and also a disaster for the front of your car.

The closer we came to the Rocky Mountains the more beautiful they appeared. Sadly, in so many of our travels we were too busy to enjoy the local sights. However, at this moment, here we were in one of the most famous spots in the world with time to enjoy it.

We booked 2 days at a reasonably-priced hotel. The hotel manager asked if we had planned to take a swim? He was joking, right? In subfreezing weather? To our surprise he explained there were hundreds of hot springs in the region.

Fortunately, we did just happen to have our swimming suits along. Many times people played tricks on us because we did not know the area, but we took a chance and donned our suits. Looking out the window of our room, sure enough, we saw the pool and people actually in it. We ventured out, tightly wrapped in coats and scarves, then threw them on a chair and jumped into the steaming water. Big snowflakes drifted onto us from the sky What an experience! I kept most of my body under the warm water. It was strange being in sub-freezing temperatures with snow landing on our heads, and yet being perfectly warm! Banff is world-famous, and yet we had never seen it. It was certainly a bonus. After having endured all the other stresses, it turned out to be a wonderful way to relax in the beautiful mountains.

Meanwhile unknown to us, Pastor Ken was on the phone contacting churches and arranging a schedule for us that filled the entire three months, leading us back eastward along the southern Canadian border. During these three months we visited larger churches, but many smaller ones as well. Some were led by pastors who were often discouraged, and filled with people who were thrilled to have the challenge and excitement of a guest evangelist, along with puppets and Bible stories for their children. Those pastors were encouraged during those months, and scores of young people dedicated their lives to Christ. God's plans were bigger than our plans. This whole experience taught us that our lives are in our Father's hands, and He is faithful.

4

✦✦✦✦✦

No Promises

"Gene, I always thought you were an intelligent young man, yet you're telling me that as you're traveling month after month, you don't have the faintest idea how much money you're going to get?"

I was in my 20's, sitting in my Uncle Ken's den in Birmingham, Alabama. Through the window I viewed his manicured lawn and gardens, stretching downhill toward a street of magnificent homes. In his garage sat both a brand-new Cadillac and a new Buick. Uncle Ken was wealthy, and he was probing, trying to figure out where I stood financially.

I was more concerned about my uncle's soul, and had been for many years. I often looked for openings to share with him eternity and the mercy and grace of God.

During our visit that day, he asked me this question, "Gene, where will you be traveling next?" I explained that our itinerary would take us across the Southern U.S. and eventually out to California. But uncle Ken had a specific purpose in asking. He continued, "Gene, how much money will you get in the next church?" I replied that I didn't know. He continued, "but what about the church after that? What will they pay you there?" I answered that I didn't know. One more time he asked, "In the third church you visit, how much will they pay you there?" And I gave the same answer, that I didn't know.

Being a prosperous businessman, he looked at me in shock. He exclaimed, "You mean you don't know how much money you're going to get in each place you visit?" He stared at me somewhat confused.

"That's right, Uncle Ken – I believe God has called us into the ministry and He will supply all our needs," I responded.

Today I still believe that *"where God guides, He provides."* After **55 years of full-time ministry, I have never had to make financial demands on any church, whether I was a guest speaker or a pastor.**

It is amazing how the Lord has supplied our needs and given us many blessings as well. One such blessing - He provided a core of financial counselors who have given us sound financial advice.

Another blessing - as long as we traveled 50 weeks a year, we had no need for a house. We stayed with my folks when we came home to Memphis. However, with a growing family the time came that we needed to buy a home. Ruby, a real estate agent, showed us a 3-bedroom, 1 ½ bath house in East Memphis. "It's too nice for us!" we exclaimed. We had often been staying in very humble settings.

"No," she insisted. "The price of this house has been greatly reduced. You have enough for a down payment, and the monthly notes on this place are low. This is the house you need, and I won't charge you real estate fees." She even saw there was no washer or drier in the house, and bought us a set! Her advice proved good, and we lived there for a year. When the time came for us to leave and go to Thailand to work with American servicemen. Ruby insisted on finding renters and caring for the house while we were gone, at no charge.

Interest rates had risen, and people were preferring to rent homes instead of buying. I was surprised to find that the rent on our home more than paid the mortgage each month. Owning rental property often necessitates re-painting and carpeting each time occupants move out. (Or are chased out for not paying their rent.) However, income from that home kept us comfortably afloat for several years no matter where we lived, whether in the States or in other countries. Later, rental income from other properties provided retirement finances for us, as we followed the advice of our counselors.

Another blessing - it was surprising to us and others that we often received far more from the churches we visited, than if we had actually "set a price on our ministry!" At one time we felt led to invest 3 months in the New England area. Most of the churches were small. Many of the pastors had to work in various secular jobs to survive. However, once again we had "bargained" with God: if He would open the doors to thriving churches, we would go anywhere else with no demands.

I recall at least 3 times that no offerings were taken during the entire weeks of services in New England. Of course, we were concerned about how we would survive during those times. Yet, each time on the final night, the pastor presented us with a generous check. When I asked how these churches could give us so much, the pastors replied that they had been saving money for weeks to be able to invite us.

You may also wonder how we were able to travel to other countries, receiving no income for months at a time, as we spoke in remote places and third world areas. When visiting churches in the States, the pastors would often take a special missionary offering for us. These gifts were sent to a restricted account in our Assemblies of God Missions Department, designated for approved overseas crusades.

We have been given much. The Bible says, "To whom much is given, much will be required." May we never forget our responsibility to bless others as we have been blessed.

5

❖ ✦ ❖ ✦ ❖

A Divinely Arranged "Accident"

It seems we "accidentally" ended up in servicemen's ministry in Thailand. Out of nowhere we received an invitation from our Missions Department. They asked if we could **go to Thailand for three months** and fill in at our Christian servicemen's center there. We had just bought a brand-new car for our lengthy road trips and all our meetings were booked across the States for nearly a year. Logically, it looked as though we were not the people for the job. It was a tough decision. The Vietnam War was at its height! Here at home anti-war demonstrations were raging, and protests and bloody riots were rampant across America. However, we prayed about God's will and what He would have us do. In doing so, we felt peace to accept the invitation to go to Thailand. We had held gospel crusades in Thailand earlier when passing through Asia. This time we were being asked to run our Bangkok Christian Servicemen's Center for a short time.

Bangkok is a city of beautiful architecture and wonderful market places full of exquisite silks and clothes, hand carved wood and ivory items. During the Vietnam War it was also a place where many men went on military leave. Unfortunately, sections of Bangkok were also dedicated to drug dens, strip clubs, brothels and bars. Their wares were enticing and cheap - everything an American GI could dream of after being at sea or in battle for months. We knew the tropical heat would be oppressive, but our greatest concern was for our servicemen and their moral and spiritual lives.

First - one big challenge! We had just six weeks to raise enough money to live on for three months plus pay for the airfare. This task seemed nearly impossible. We did have a group of churches across the US that had supported our overseas ministry over the years. Once again, those folks gave generously, allowing us to leave for Bangkok on time.

On one of our first nights in Bangkok, I found that among my new duties was hosting a prayer meeting with Roman Catholics. **This was a meeting of Roman Catholic priests and nuns** and a few servicemen stationed there in the capital city. To be honest, ministering to Roman Catholics for the first time was somewhat intimidating, because many Catholics had been taught it was a sin to attend a Protestant gathering. Yet these people were so gracious. Among those in this group were Father O'Brien, a Roman Catholic priest, and three nuns. It was a delight to talk to them, study the Bible, and pray with them.

Father O'Brien had one request: we pray for him that he might receive the Holy Spirit baptism. I had never prayed for a Roman Catholic priest before. I did not know whether to place my hands on his shoulders or his head or not touch him at all, so it was a new experience for me. I prayerfully placed my hands on his head and began to pray, "Dear Father, bless Father, um. . ." I stopped and tried again. "Dear Father, bless Father," and finally – "Oh Lord, just pour out your Spirit upon my friend." He seemed unperturbed by my stumbling prayer, and the presence of God was electric. We also prayed with each of the nuns.

Interestingly, in the 1960's there had been a great outpouring of the Holy Spirit among Catholics, world-wide. This outpouring of the Holy Spirit reached a peak in the Notre Dame football stadium when thousands of people gathered to seek the Lord. This miraculous movement continued to spread from there to Catholic parishes abroad, especially in South America. At one time, there had been a great deal of persecution of Protestants in South America, but the Holy Spirit was beginning to bridge the spiritual gap. It is quite amazing to note that Roman Catholics were far more receptive to the Holy Spirit baptism, with the evidence of speaking in other tongues, than traditional Protestants.

Many fine main-line Protestant churches teach that the miracles, speaking in other tongues, supernatural healings, etc. described in the Book of Acts (chapter 2) would no longer be experienced after the Early Church era. The *initial* outpouring of the Holy Spirit happened on the Day of Pentecost, as recorded in the Book Acts. People who considered that such things still occur today became known as Pentecostals and were often considered simply over-emotional worshipers. At present, the Pentecostal believers have become the fastest growing Christian group in the world. Roman Catholic Pentecostals are referred to as "Charismatic Catholics," and the fervor of many of them continues to this day. Something very deep and meaningful was happening in the lives of these people we worshiped with in Thailand.

We were only scheduled to be in Bangkok for three months. During that time, we met with various servicemen's groups. One of the amusing things that happened there involved a group of 4 American airmen. They had gotten themselves stranded in Bangkok with no money or change of clothes. These guys were stationed several thousand miles off the coast of Thailand on a top-secret island base on Diego Garcia. Few people have heard of this base in the Indian Ocean. It had been shrouded in secrecy because of it being a nuclear submarine harbor and also a B52 bomber base.

Only one flight a week went from Diego Garcia to Bangkok. These 4 men had missed a flight back to their base. Now they were stuck in Bangkok, had wasted their money on nightlife, and had nowhere to go.

Somehow, they found their way to the Bangkok Christian Servicemen's Center. They told us they were stranded for a week and had no food and nowhere to stay. It was obvious that they did not come to the center to seek spiritual help. This bunch was rowdy and anything but godly.

We fed them and gave them a place to sleep. Our center provided activities at night, but we contemplated what to do with the guys during the day. Our work was just beginning, and we were not yet familiar with tourist spots. Heather said "Hey, why don't I take them down to the local meat market and give them a taste of what Thailand is really like? They can carry the groceries."

She took the men down to the local market. It was a big open square area about the size of a city block. Wooden poles supported corrugated tin roofs, sheltering parts of the area from the hot sun. Piles of colorful fruits and vegetables were stacked pyramid-style on plastic sheets on the bare ground. People milled around the produce, laughing, chatting with the sales people and bargaining for the best prices. Further back among the stalls, the roofs had come to an end and canvas cloths were stretched overhead in their place. When the group passed the fish stalls. Heather noticed our American men almost gagging from the smell. They continued on to the meat section where people were butchering chickens and small animals. Slabs of raw pork and beef hung from hooks overhead. Even water buffalo was available for purchase. The stench of blood was revolting, made even worse by the heat. Heather could see these tough, macho-acting Seabees were fighting nausea by then, as she struggled to keep a straight face. In amusement she pinched a hunk of beef between her fingers to check its tenderness just to aggravate them further, and finally led them back to our center.

We were able to share the message of salvation with these men, and pray with them. At the end of the week, we took the men to the airport where they caught the routine military flight back to Diego Garcia.

Another unusual incident occurred, also involving a stranded U.S. airman. He arrived at our center in flip flops, torn jeans, no shirt, and needing a place to spend the night. He related to us the sad story of what happened to the rest of his clothes and wallet. He had come to Bangkok to have a "good time," and somehow had gotten involved with a Thai "girlfriend." Sometime during the night in their hotel room, he had decided to take a shower. After the shower, he was shocked to find his "girlfriend" gone, along with all his clothes and his wallet. She had thrown his belongings out the window to a waiting accomplice and disappeared. I suppose he had gone to the front desk dressed only in a towel, and the manager had found an old bathrobe for him to wear. Needless to say, his happy time in Bangkok was over.

During the Viet Nam War, many of our American men hooked up with prostitutes as soon as they landed in Bangkok. Many of these girls were looking for a ticket to America. Some of them had been lured from small country towns to the city by an "agent" who had promised them a good job. Most "agents" were simply pimps. Either way, multitudes of young women ended up becoming prostitutes and drug pushers after arriving in Bangkok. Our men who were lonely were looking for love and affection in the wrong places. They had not heard the words of King Solomon, "The lips of an immoral woman are as sweet as honey and her mouth is smoother than oil. But in the end she is a bitter poison, as dangerous as a double-edged sword. Her feet go down to death..." (Proverbs 5:4) Usually both the lives of our servicemen and the lives of these young women were destroyed during those encounters.

Now after 3 months had passed, we were ready to return to the States – until another surprise invitation arrived. Would we consider leading a servicemen's center in **UTAPAO near the American Air Force base 100 miles away?** This was the last place on earth anyone would want to be! If we accepted that invitation, we would certainly be venturing where few have dared to go. But we'll save that adventure for another chapter.

6

✦✦✦✦

Navigating the Hazards of Bangkok

Driving in Bangkok is like driving nowhere else. It is not for the faint-hearted. Traffic delays and tie-ups are so bad on the streets of Bangkok it may take an hour to go 3 or 4 blocks. Many drivers wait until 2:00 to 4:00 AM to venture on a trip through the city.

GRAFFITI?

On our first journey from the airport into the city, we noticed what seemed to be a couple of white spray-painted outlines of men sprawled on the black asphalt of the main street. The next day we noticed the same thing in other places, along with a few shapes of cars and motorcycles outlined in white on the blacktop. Was this some crude graffiti sprayed on the roads by bored teens? The artists, we were told, were actually not teens, but police officers. After a traffic accident on a busy street, the police simply sprayed an outline of the vehicles and/or passengers on the pavement, then quickly cleared the wreckage out of the way of traffic. Later they photographed the outlines and used them in police investigations and insurance settlements. So, every morning we could read the events of the night before sprayed on the pavement of the streets. It was unnerving to drive down the thoroughfares and to see these white etchings of motorbike and auto crashes, usually fatal, outlined on the black pavement.

PARKING IN BANGKOK? NO PROBLEM!

All Bangkok parking lots were crowded. One day a friend was driving me to an appointment. When he pulled into the parking lot, all the parking slots were filled. "NO PROBLEM," he assured me. He slid into a small space behind a car, totally hemming in the other vehicle. When another vehicle pulled in behind us, leaving barely a foot between us, he laughed. Still, "NO PROBLEM," he said. "The custom is, you get as close as possible to the cars around you until there is no way they can maneuver their way out."

We got out and he shut and locked the door. "You may even lock your car," he continued, "BUT be sure to leave your car in neutral. When the drivers around you find they cannot move, they just push your car out of their way and no one gets upset."

I just shook my head. Incredible! But I am pretty sure if we had forgotten to put our car in neutral, there could have been a *major* problem. Someone would have had to wait until we returned, and would have been steaming mad at our thoughtlessness. However, the system seemed to work, especially since many of the cars had hired drivers, who did the pushing as part of their job.

ONE WRECK TOO MANY

During the time we lived in Bangkok, we became acquainted with a new missionary who had just arrived from Canada. He was delighted that his mission board had provided him with a car. However, on the very first day while trying to get the hang of driving on the left side of the road, he had a wreck. Bangkok traffic could be terrifying to a newcomer, and the reckless way they drove had shaken him up. Even when traffic became snarled and slow, literally hundreds of motorcycles constantly whizzed in and out between the cars and buses, some with their wives and even children on the back of the motor bikes. (I swear the drivers in Bangkok must get their licenses out of a CORN FLAKE box.)

Unfortunately, 2 weeks later my friend had another accident. I guarantee that Tom (not his real name) was a cautious driver, but found driving in Bangkok a nightmare.

Tom was having a struggle, not just with the traffic but with the Thai language. Both he and I had been assigned to the language class for "dummies". That meant that no matter how hard we tried, we were way behind the other students. But at least I'm very proud of one thing. I became fluent enough in Thai to be able to ask *"Where are the bathrooms?"*

Unfortunately, about three weeks later Tom had a third wreck. None of these were serious, but they did shake him up. Since some police officers could be intimidating while investigating an accident, there was no way for a foreigner to anticipate what officers might do. The language barrier further complicated the situation for a newcomer. The more frustrated an officer became trying to communicate with a foreigner, the louder he tended to yell to get his message across.

Tom was struggling to learn the Thai language and was doing the best he could. I understood how he felt as I also struggled with the Thai language, one of the most difficult in the world. Thai is a tonal language. So you might want to say, "Did you eat the *rice* yet?" Instead, you could easily be saying, "Did you eat *him* yet," simply by lowering the tone of your voice on the exact same Thai word.

As I spoke with Tom, he put his head in his hands and said to me, "If I have another wreck I'm packing up and going home." I prayed for him. He was an extremely gifted man in many ways and got along well with the local people. I hated for him to be so disappointed, but that same week Tom had another minor collision. The next day Tom had his belongings packed, booked a flight, and took his family back to Canada.

The Thai language is tough for many people. I worked on it day and night. I recorded all of my classes on tape and I listened to them constantly - driving home from the language school, at my desk at home, and on family trips. I believe I almost drove my family nuts, listening to me trying to pronounce the complex tones of the language while they were in the car with me. On the other hand, Heather seemed to be born with a natural gift for learning language. This was so disgusting because I struggled so hard. I must admit I hated every minute of class and she enjoyed it!

While in Bangkok, I served for a time as administrator of our Bangkok Theological Seminary. I could communicate a little, but unfortunately, I had to lean on interpreters too much. I made a vow that if I could learn Thai well enough to preach in it without an interpreter, then we would stay in Thailand. So, I gave it all I had. Eventually we decided to leave! It seemed the Lord had different plans for us, though we were sad to say "Goodbye."

7

Don't Go There! And Definitely Not Alone!

One day I met a young, enthusiastic missionary in Thailand who had been in Bangkok for about a year. I'll call him Bob. When I asked what his main ministry was, he boasted, "I work in the brothels among the prostitutes." Shocked, I paused a moment. Then I inquired what part his wife played in this unusual ministry.

His response was disturbing. "I go to the bars and my wife stays home with our children." My heart sank. I had seen such risky behavior among well-meaning Christian men several times.

Because I was concerned for him, I explained how many dedicated young Christian men had fallen into the trap of Satan by attempting to minister in this way. The riskiest thing he, or anyone could do was to have contact with any of these "girls of the evening" without a coworker present. With a slight smirk, he arrogantly assured me that he was a strong enough Christian to handle any temptation.

Several weeks passed before Heather and I were back in Bangkok, and this time we happened to meet Bob's wife. "How is Bob doing?" I asked. His wife teared up. "He has 'fallen in love' with one of the prostitutes and our mission has ordered us back HOME!"

Oh, how many times have I heard the boasting of pride and over-confidence by well-meaning people. Sexual sin happens all too often even among professing Christians. Satan can lure both men and women into affairs even in the church world. Pastors themselves have fallen into adultery. Sometimes this begins with only a casual, private conversation. At other times what starts out as "counseling" has ended up in sexual intimacy.

Unfortunately, pornography has also crept into the lives of Christians in America and around the world with the ease of clicking onto the internet. Even children are targeted and lured into its net before parents realize what's happening.

A few years ago at a church men's retreat, 80% of the fellows who attended the retreat admitted that pornography had gotten a hold on them. During a time of prayer and confession, these men banded together and agreed confidentially to keep in touch and hold each other accountable in the following days. One of the most notable results of the agreement was that the confession was kept confidential and no one outside the group ever knew about it. In the months following the retreat, these men bonded together closely as true brothers, and held each other's feet to the fire for their commitment - with great success!

Many years ago, as Billy Graham began his ministry, he was shocked to see even good people fall in this way. Early in Mr. Graham's ministry he made it a point to surrounded himself with a core of Godly men. Together they prayed about how they could make agreements that would help them sustain the integrity their ministry. One part of a covenant they made together was a pledge to never meet a woman alone for any reason. While so many other good teams of men had fallen into disgrace, the men that teamed with Graham for decades never had any shadows cast over their ministry due to inappropriate behavior.

Another outstanding Christian organization frankly discussed the pitfalls of working closely with those of the opposite sex. They made a stipulation that while traveling on any out-of-town trip with someone of the opposite sex, they would each drive in separate cars. While seemingly inconvenient and expensive for 2 people to follow each other on a road trip, they felt this was a safeguard. Over the years this group has also maintained its reputation for integrity.

Bonding with people who love us and pray with us as we face so many temptations, is a great safeguard for building strong Christian character and avoiding tragedy.

8

·····◆·◆·◆·◆·◆·····

Floods, Alligators, and Cobras

OOPS! A MAJOR MISTAKE

Several years after that first assignment in Bangkok, we returned for a 2-year assignment as director of our Bible school there. By then, our baby daughter, Deborah, had grown into a lovely 13-year-old. I tried to figure what our teenage daughter would like for her birthday. I had always enjoyed taking out-of-country guests to the ALLIGATOR FARM in Bangkok. There, the reptiles are kept in pits of various dimensions depending on the creatures' sizes. Tourists pay to watch men wrestle the alligators – an exciting afternoon for our visiting friends! Adjoining shops sell alligator hides and meat.

I had also taken many visitors to the COBRA FARM to watch the cobras being "milked." Official-looking men in white coats would move among a pit full of cobras. With only a large spoon, they would torment the cobras, enticing them to strike and release their venom. All of the venom was collected in a container and given to the RED CROSS. Then the venom was injected into a water buffalo that produced cobra antibodies for vaccines.

There were literally thousands of cobras in the city, and during the heavy rains of flood season there were even more in the yards and streets. Every year people die from cobra bites. Even in the murky water, you may see these snakes swimming around your yard in rainy season. Today, in our "museum" we have a 7-foot-long cobra skin bought on the streets of Bangkok, reminding us of those floods.

Since I wanted to do something exciting and different for Deborah's 13th birthday, I hit on the idea of taking her, along with Som and Heather, to the cobra farm. Boy, was I out of touch with what teen-age daughters liked! This time I STRUCK OUT BIG TIME with Debbie. However, she bravely watched the huge disgusting snakes being "milked." Later we all enjoyed a lovely birthday dinner at an elegant hotel.

THE FLOODS

The most terrifying aspect of living in Bangkok was enduring the annual floods when all the streets and sidewalks were covered with water. It was difficult to tell exactly what we could be stepping on. We had found it hard to believe all the "flood stories" we had heard. But the first time we saw the waters rise and Bangkok flooded, we understood. That first morning I went out to get into our car to drive to our Bible school, *Bangkok Theological Seminary*. The water had risen up over the fenders of the car. Inside, the driver's seat was covered with water! Even though it seemed hopeless, I attempted to start the car while sitting in the water. Can you believe, it started up immediately? We had to raise the hood so that the fan belt would not fling water back into the motor and drown it.

Once the car was started, the next major problem was to figure out where the street was. Klongs ran along both sides of the road even in normal times. Klongs, or deep ditches, flowed throughout the city to carry off excess waste water. In other words, they were actually open smelly sewers that ran beside the streets. As I nervously started the trip to our Bible school, I asked a young neighborhood boy to sit on our fender where he could look down and see where the pavement stopped and the klong began. and to guide me along through the water. He had already helped several other drivers stay on the road out to the main street. When we got out of the deepest water, he asked for a tip and went on to help other stranded vehicles.

Just down the street was a car that had slipped into a klong. In a few more yards I came to a major intersection. A brave Volkswagen driver had dared to enter the intersection in the rising water. The VW is supposed to be water-tight and I guess it was. In the middle of the intersection was a hilarious sight - the little VW was bobbing helplessly up and down like a cork, water-tight but unable to get traction!

My concern now was our Bible school. It had flooded in the past. And if it flooded again, since I was now the director, I would be the one who was supposed to "fix" things. On my arrival at the school, I was relieved to find that industrious faculty and students had placed sand bags around the major buildings. There was no flooding inside our school!

Bangkok is situated on the coast of Thailand. By late afternoon as the ocean tide receded, the flooding in the city eased. Now we were left with foul-smelling wet upholstery in our car. The flood waters were filthy and the insides of the car soon began to mildew. The only option was to consult our car insurance company and take the vehicle to an interior repair shop to get the upholstery stripped and replaced. For 2 weeks we really missed not having a car. Bangkok did fortunately have a fairly good public transportation system. The buses were the best and only way to get around in the flood season. And even though their enormous wheels lifted the floor of the buses high off the road, water still came up to the passengers' feet and flowed up and down the aisles.

When we got our car back the rains had eased, but areas of the city were still flooded. And would you believe, about 3 weeks after enjoying our re-conditioned car, there came an extremely heavy storm and the water rose over our fenders again. So back we went to the upholstery shop to get the interior fabric ripped out and replaced again.

In the period of heavy rains, the locals found various ways to cope with the floods. People carried little bags with them on the buses and when walking in flooded areas. In each bag they would resourcefully put a change of clothes, pair of socks, rubber shoes, plus a small bottle of cleanser. We soon learned to do the same.

As new missionaries, we had been concerned about getting lost in a huge city in which we did not know the language or customs. However, some of the biggest challenges that confronted us were not our ignorance of language, or even possible tropical diseases, or terrorist attacks, but the floods and cobras during rainy season. But we learned to cope with it all, and to love the wonderful Thai people and their beautiful country.

9

A Contract on My Life

AN INVITATION TO "HELL"

Would anyone like to live with no electricity in 90 degree weather, surrounded by piles of garbage, bars, brothels and drug dens? After our 3-month tour in Bangkok, we were eager to get back to America. Just before we left Thailand, our Missions Department received an urgent message that a group of airmen stationed in a remote area about 70 miles south of Bangkok wanted help establishing a servicemen center. Ten thousand Americans were stationed there at a vast US bomber base called UTAPAO. A small group of Christian men had been meeting in a broken-down shed across from the main gate of the base. They had already brought many of their friends to the Lord. Now they needed a full-time leader to move into the area and provide a home-like atmosphere where they could worship, bring friends, eat, and spend their off-duty hours.

Our Missions Department urged us to "just take a look at the area." Out of courtesy, we went to survey the situation. What we saw was so depressing, my immediate inclination was to hop back on a bus for Bangkok and return to Memphis ASAP.

The spiritual need was obvious. Many of our servicemen had become addicted to hard drugs. A giggling group of scantily clad "ladies of the evening" constantly hung around the main gate to the base. These girls would call out to our men using the few English words they knew: "Hey you! You movie star? Wow! You look same-same movie star!" They'd often throw in some vulgar words they had learned from the fellows. As our men left the base after their shifts, these scantily clad women would actually grab at the shirts of some of the men. The whole environment was rotten. It would take a very strong young man to resist the women and drugs. Unfortunately, a great number of our airmen developed V.D, including some incurable strains, during their term of duty at Utapao.

After looking over the area and talking with some of the Christian men, we gave a vague promise to pray about it. I distinctly remember kneeling beside our bed and praying, "Lord, this place needs a missionary. Please send somebody!" It was during that prayer that something gripped my heart, and I felt overwhelmed by the sense that we were the ones who were supposed to go.

INITIATION OF A BRAND NEW SERVICEMEN'S CENTER

With the help of a dedicated corps of men, we rented a 4-room concrete block building in the middle of the bars, brothels, drug dens, and garbage piles. We wanted to make this building as nice as possible for our men so far from home. **This, our first center was certainly not fancy.** We bought some locally made wicker furniture. It was more comfortable than sitting on the bare paint-splattered concrete floor. And that floor certainly needed some attention as well - like a new paint job!

One day, hoping to find some concrete paint, I hopped on a little open-sided bus and rode down to the only hardware store in the area. I tried to explain to the owner that I needed some enamel paint for our floor. I chose a pleasant shade of blue. Heather and I worked several hours painting the floor with what was supposed to be permanent concrete paint.

We could hardly wait until our first guests showed up. The floor was such an improvement over all of those discolorations. Unfortunately, our thrills and excitement did not last very long. As soon as the first airmen arrived and walked across the floor, the so-called permanent paint came off onto the bottom of the men's shoes and left tracks everywhere. It's hard to describe exactly how I felt. First of all, I'd never heard of concrete paint coming off, and secondly, we had spent all of our available money for this wonderful durable enamel. Since I did not know what to do, I did what every real man does, I got blazing mad. I loaded the remaining paint cans on another little bus, took them back to the hardware store and placed them on the counter. The owner did not speak much English and that's probably just as well, because I wasn't really able to inform her in Thai what was on my mind. The only way to express my disappointment and anger was to say to her, "You are 'number 10' (an insulting Thai expression) for lying to me about the paint quality." I learned later that what I had said was almost as bad as murder. I had insulted her. I did get my money back, but only by speaking to this store owner in a very non-Christian way. Since she did not speak much English all she knew was that I was very upset.

I found out that evening that one of the worst things one can do in Thailand is to lose one's temper. I did not lose my temper, but I got within a half inch of it. Back at the center that night a car pulled up on our dirt road in the dark. The Thai man who got out spoke perfect English. The owner of the hardware store had put a contract on my life, he said. I had insulted her to the degree that she lost face and wanted me dead. For those of us in the West, this is inconceivable. Yet, in that crime-ridden area, there were Thai Mafia-type hit men that could be hired in cases like this. The wealthier the intended victim, the higher the bounty. I'm not sure where I fit on that scale, but I realized I had seriously violated a cultural norm. The only thing I could do was to eat a giant piece of humble pie.

I rushed back to the hardware store in a panic, with a good interpreter and explained that I was sorry for whatever I had said that was rude. This is one of the things I write about that I certainly am not proud of. I took the owner a gift and explained again that I was just a dumb foreigner. Certainly, it is possible the owner did not really understand the kind of paint I wanted. Be that as it may, I made a terrible cultural mistake and was determined it would never happen again.

In the end we covered the floor with a huge rattan rug, making the room appear comfortable, neat and inviting. The only thing the men objected to then was the restroom.

The main fixture in the bathroom was a hole in the concrete floor with blocks on each side to stand on. Yes, stand. There was nothing to sit on. Such facilities are common in third world countries. The fixture was polished white ceramic and clean, but the guys hated it. Oh yes, there was a tiled reservoir in one corner filled with water. The user flushed the unit with a dipperful of water from the reservoir. A few wives who had accompanied their husbands on this remote tour almost fainted when they saw the restroom. Something had to be done. Heather found a cartoon of a fellow scratching his head in confusion. She pasted it on the wall, along with "user instructions." It was the best we could do as we strove to make a home for these men so far from their families.

10

✦✦✦✦

Making the Electric Meter Run Backwards

Moving is always a daunting challenge, whether you move across town or you move to a new city. However, moving our family halfway around the world to Thailand involved facing totally different challenges. These challenges included having to learn a completely new language, trying to figure out their local monetary system and struggling to understand literally scores of new customs and ways of doing things that seemed uncomfortably strange, even bizarre.

One of the most challenging things we had to do was to find a larger building for our servicemen's center and home for our family. The home the servicemen had originally rented quickly became too cramped. We had decided to rent a newer building in what may be called a tiny community, if by "community" you mean a cluster of brothels, drug dens, garbage piles, and gang hangouts. If you speak a common language and your customs are somewhat similar, then negotiating a lease is relatively simple. Unfortunately, this certainly was not the case in this unique community in Thailand.

I found out I was in trouble from square one, since I did not speak the language and those who claimed they did speak English certainly did not understand it. Yet, we signed a lease with the landlord for a large two-story building. The landlord was a little fellow with shifty eyes and a big innocent smile. The girl we had hired as a maid, hated him.

We moved our family into an upstairs apartment. Two other military families moved into the other upstairs apartments and paid us rent, which helped with building expenses. Downstairs was a big meeting room and kitchen.

When the electric bills for our new center came due, the cost seemed astonishing for the amount of electricity we were using. Was it possible our neighbors had somehow tapped into our electrical wiring? Such shenanigans were fairly normal in that area of the country. In order to determine how much power we were actually using, we decided to shut off all our electricity for a few minutes. Guess what? Our electric meter kept spinning. I had complained to our landlord that something was wrong with the electric bill being so huge. He had nodded, smiled, and said he would check on it. Yet, nothing changed.

Thus, I hired another electrician to check our meter. He inspected the box, made a few adjustments and left. The next month when the utility company checked our meter, the reading registered *below* the previous month's usage. The meter reader shook his head and left. The following month the reading was *still lower* than the previous month.

Now came a big explosion between the electric company and our landlord. The agent for the electric company was furious. He and the landlord came to me to sort out the problem. I explained I had been complaining about the huge electric bills and our landlord had done nothing about it. As a result, I hired another electrician who claimed to have fixed our meter for us. I declared I had no idea of what went wrong.

Guess what? The electric company also discovered that all the wiring from the houses behind us had been routed through our meter. Our landlord sheepishly agreed to have our meter rewired. I was ready to choke the landlord, but I was laughing too hard. New meters were quickly installed in each separate house. It's a game in that part of the world: "Do unto others before they can do it to you. Then act innocent when caught," which is what our landlord did with our electricity.

P.S. Our landlord later served a term as a Buddhist monk. Our Buddhist maid had to bow to the little fellow whenever he came around the center. As for us – no, we didn't bow. No way!

11

Green Slime Showers

The new building we had rented for the servicemen's center sat a few yards back from the highway across from the Air Force base in Thailand. An open field separated our building from a restaurant beside us that was mainly a bar. In the middle of the field between us was a huge open cistern, or well, almost hidden by a sea of tall grass and trash.

BUT WHAT ABOUT EXCESSIVE WATER BILLS?

The next time a local plumber came by, I asked him to explain where the pipes ran that brought to water to our building. He hesitated, shrugged, and pointed vaguely to the gravel road that ran up a small hill behind our center. Along the little road sat wooden houses on stilts occupied by local prostitutes, along with a shack that passed for a beauty shop, and a Thai noodle shop.

When I questioned him further, the plumber finally said that I could just follow the pipes running from the cistern. Cistern? Our water was coming from the big open pit in the field? Some of the pipes *were* visible. They were difficult to follow, but I soon figured out that the meter on the side of our house was measuring all the water used by the entire neighborhood up the hill behind our building, and it was coming from the cistern. I was stunned. We were paying for everyone's water! I could have complained, but why bother? The water bill was relatively small. I chuckled and walked away, feeling I was in a constant game of "who can outsmart who?"

It was not until after we moved in that we noticed the water coming from our faucets was filthy. At first it was just great to find out we actually had a shower in the bathroom. When we first turned on the shower, not much happened. Gradually, tiny streams of greenish water began to trickle out of the shower head. Before long the water was accompanied by long strands of green algae. We wondered where this gunk was coming from. I went back outside and followed the pipes going toward the bar next door. It was then I noticed there was a water reservoir on the roof of the bar. That reservoir was obviously serving as a water tower for the neighborhood.

Out of curiosity I climbed up the side of the building and looked over into the tank. That is when I realized the water provided to us was being pumped up from the open cistern in the field to this open concrete reservoir. Also, the cistern was simply a huge muddy pit in the ground filled with rainwater, along with algae and other trash. Thus, the water being pumped up into the reservoir was leaving a layer of mud on the bottom of the concrete tank. Unfortunately, that made all the water going into our house murky and green.

In a way I wish I had not looked, for what we thought was simply muddy water was at least 50% green slime. Sadly, this slimy water was the source of all of the water going into our building. I had never seen a sight like this before. It kind of freaked me out and I wondered how to fix it.

I know at various times in the States, we used Clorox in our laundry and even to scrub our tile floors. So, I thought, why not get a few gallons of Clorox mixed with water to scrub out this reservoir and see if that would eliminate, or at least reduce, our algae problem. I went to town and, yes, back to the same hardware store where the lady had gotten so mad at me. However, this time I tried my charm on her. I bought all of the Clorox she had in stock and took it back to Utapao. I was able to clean out most of the green sludge with a shovel, add more water, and then add bleach to the tank. (I missed the class in seminary on how to deal with things like this.)

Now it was time to see if my Clorox experiment would work. I think it was rare for local Thais to see an American work so hard and actually sweat. Plus, they probably wondered what I was doing on top of the restaurant building. I do know that the restaurant employees gasped when they saw the Clorox containers with the skull and crossbones pictured on the sides. Though they could not read the English labels, they certainly knew what the "poison" logo meant. So, the rumor went around the area that the Americans wanted to poison the entire community. Also, the laundry workers at the bar next door complained the water smelled like bleach.

Up to this time everyone in the area boiled their own water to kill bacteria - even our missionaries did this. Of course, kitchens in the tropics were hot already, and boiling the water made everything hotter. Afterwards, several Americans began following my simple formula of putting a few drops of Clorox into their water instead of boiling it. This saved much effort and helped keep their kitchens from getting incredibly hot! Further, they realized that in America the city water supply is *routinely* chlorinated. This was not a revolutionary idea!

From this time onward, we had relatively clean water and no more green slimy showers! Now, onward to the next challenge. We were surely venturing where few would dare or want to go, nor would we have chosen to go there ourselves. Unexpected shocks constantly kept us off balance.

12

Thai Bar Girls Cuss in Perfect English

One day I was riding on a local baht bus - one of the colorful open-sided little vehicles that cost one baht, or 5 cents to ride. As I climbed aboard, I heard some of the local Thai "party girls" cussing in perfect English. Several thoughts burst into my mind: If these girls could cuss in English, maybe they could learn to converse in it as well as just swear in it. Possibly we could hold English classes in our servicemen's center? I felt that a simple English Bible story book would make an excellent text book! The idea began to take shape.

To carry out the plan, I first needed a Thai partner who was a true Christian and could communicate in both Thai and English. A fellow Assemblies of God missionary recommended I speak with Brother Preecha. Preecha was a wonderful young man - a converted Buddhist priest and recent graduate from our Bible school. When I first talked with him about my idea, he was able to speak very little English. To make matters more complicated, I spoke very little Thai. Needless to say we had few arguments.

Our servicemen's center, The Vine, contained a large room completely surrounded on two sides with tall windows. We had equipped it with a ping pong table, couches, and plenty of folding tables and chairs. To prepare for the classes we set up a few tables and some chairs, and announced we were open for business – English lessons two nights a week.

The US airmen who frequented the center were eager to be the teachers. They spoke with a variety of accents depending on where they were from in the States. We were amused to hear the southern fellows using slang such as, "y'all" and "ain't," and throwing in an extra syllable on some words. This promised to be an interesting venture.

In the beginning, we had only 3 students – 3 young Thai men reveling in the personal attention of these rich American teachers. (Thais figured all Americans were rich.) The news spread. It wasn't long before we had 25 students, all eager to learn.

From the first, we decided that if the classes were totally free, the students would not appreciate the school. Thus, we settled on a token fee of about 25 cents a month. The fee included a simple English Bible story book as a text book, and periodic refreshments.

As we planned the school schedule, we decided Pastor Preecha would give a brief devotion mid-way through each one-hour class. These students had no knowledge of the Bible. Most of our students had never heard the name of Jesus, except in profanity! They had never heard that Jesus gave His life on the cross so that they might be ready for eternity with Him in heaven. There was no other Christian ministry for over 1,400 sq. miles from our center. The American men were excited to do real missionary work in a real foreign country. To know they were making an eternal difference in the lives of their students gave them a sense of purpose they had never experienced before.

In Thailand, less than one-half of 1% of the people were Christians. Almost all of them were Buddhists, but most of them rarely went to a Buddhist temple. Some did wear a Buddhist charm around their necks for good luck. Their goal in life was to try to do more good deeds than bad, and just hope that the forces that govern the afterlife would allow them to be reincarnated into something desirable in their next cycle of life on Earth. So, you can understand what a challenge it was to teach the simple plan of salvation to folks who had been taught something so different.

The students were mainly teenagers. They enjoyed singing songs like "Oh How I Love Jesus," and went around singing it outside of class, whether they believed in Him yet or not. Little by little, it seemed a light would turn on in their souls.

The school grew. Eventually enrollment reached 100. The classes proved popular as social gathering times for both the Thais and their American teachers. In this impoverished area, many families of these students had not been able to pay the minimal public-school fees as their children were growing up. Most of these students had dropped out of school at about the 3rd grade. Interestingly, our classes helped them improve their general education as well as increase their skills in English. Yet, our mission and passion was for them to give their hearts to Christ. Our secondary goal was that from this group of new believers would come a Thai church led by Pastor Preecha! It would be a church that would remain long after the Vietnam War was over and the Americans had left.

JOE'S STORY

It was not long before it became clear that we had more young women than young men in the school. And some of the girls appeared more interested in getting the attention of their male GI teachers than they were in learning the Bible or even English. Most of the GI teachers were in their early 20's. These men were tempting targets for those girls who had ulterior motives. And as for the young men who were the instructors, this was the first time many of them had been away from home. There in Thailand they could do exactly as they pleased for the first time in their lives. Needless to say, we often warned the men of the constant temptation of sexual immorality. As you might guess, our warnings were not always taken seriously, although most of the men who taught English remained true to the Lord during their tour of duty.

Among the young men who became active in the language school was an extremely talented guy. We'll call him Joe – a tall handsome dark-haired fellow full of self-confidence. He had been to Bible School, and was proud of it. One day during a discussion he arrogantly assured me he knew the Bible better than I did.

As I watched him teach English, I noticed Joe seemed to pay a lot of attention to one of the Thai women students. I tried to make him aware that he was being overly friendly with her. Gradually, Joe became more irregular in our chapel attendance. Then he just seemed to disappear. I heard rumors that he had moved in with one of the prostitutes. This was hard to believe because he had been to Bible school and knew better as a believer!

In my ministry at The Vine Servicemen's Center, I often tried to connect with servicemen living around the base by going door to door, chatting with them, and inviting them to the center for free home-cooked meals. For those who came for a meal, I'd usually lead in a brief conversation about the Lord after we ate. Most of them seemed to have pressing appointments that prevented them from staying long and would soon disappear.

One day I was making my usual rounds in the area where many GI's hung out with the prostitutes. I knocked lightly on one door. Around the door frame were tacked sexy pictures from old Playboy Magazines. The scantily clad girl inside barely opened the door a crack.

I had a feeling she had someone with her she did not want me to see. I gently pushed the door to glimpse inside. Guess who was sitting on the bed? JOE, THE BIBLE EXPERT! Even though it was quite obvious what was happening, he said something like, "Hi! We are having a Bible study!" I was so shocked I almost laughed.

Again, we lost contact with Joe. A rumor surfaced that one of the inmates in the regional Thai prison resembled him. I did not really believe the rumor, but I made the 45 minute trip to the prison just to check that it was not Joe. The holding cells of the regional prison were nothing more than wire cages. They called these cells, "monkey cages." I guess it was because these steel structures are so small prisoners barely had room to stand or move around in them. Such cages were similar to the ones the Viet Cong were using to imprison our captured American soldiers just across the border.

The officials confirmed that indeed Joe had been there, but had just been transferred to the military prison back at Utapao.

Still somewhat in disbelief, I went back to the base prison at Utapao. My footsteps echoed as I walked down to a cell at the end of a long hall. There, sitting on a bunk was a dejected looking young man. He had lost weight, and he was hunched over – too ashamed to look up. Unfortunately for Joe, it was now time to "reap his wild oats." The first thing he said to me were the words I have heard many times, "I never thought this could happen to me!"

Joe had been charged by the Thai authorities with possession and selling heroin. The government was very tough on drug dealers. Sad to say, there was a great deal of corruption in the Thai justice system. The normal sentence for drug dealing was life in prison with no parole. Unfortunately, I know of numerous cases in which officials planted drugs on someone and then returned later to arrest them.

Joe's parents hired the best lawyers available. After all the lengthy negotiations that ensued, the Thai prosecutor finally concluded that there could be some flexibility in Joe's life sentence. This would require the payment of a huge "fine!"

In reality this so-called fine was nothing but a bribe. The money from such penalties was usually divided between the judge and local attorneys. Most foreigners caught in this trap had little money to pay such excessive amounts. As a result, the prisoners rotted in awful Thai prisons, surviving on 1 meal of rice a day.

The "happy ending" of Joe's story was that his parents found the necessary money required to pay his "fine." The last I heard was that Joe had been released from the Utapao Base prison, given a dishonorable discharge, and the Thai government had deported him back to the States.

DID THE THAI BAR GIRLS EVER LEARN TO CONVERSE IN ENGLISH?

Joe's story was unique during those "language school" days. Most of the American "teachers" faithfully spent their spare time and effort sharing the Gospel with their Thai students, and many of the students, including bar girls, were saved. One of our frequent prayers was that the Lord would close the brothels, bars and drug dens that surrounded the American Air Force base and would one day raise up a thriving, self-supporting Thai church.

After the close of the Vietnam War, we were able to return to that area briefly. The base was closed. The bars surrounding it were abandoned and had fallen into disrepair. In their place was a thriving Thai Assembly of God church led by Pastor Preecha, my original Thai co-worker. Not only was the church still thriving, but some of the people who had been saved at The Vine had moved to the nearby coastal resort town of Pattaya to get hotel jobs. Earlier, missionary Bruce Mumm and I had purchased strategic property just off the beach in Pattaya. On that property we found that Pastor Preecha had designed and built a beautiful modern place of worship, with the help of the new believers there.

We also discovered that the original congregation, *including former bar girls* from The Vine, had established a *third* flourishing church in a town a few miles to the north of Pattaya. Three thriving churches, initially begun through the efforts of American servicemen!

Five years later I took a group of Memphis friends on a tour of Southeast Asia. Many in the group had helped fund our ministry to servicemen during the Vietnam War. I took them to see the church in Pattaya which their efforts had helped establish. They sat in the folding chairs looking around in awe, some with tears in their eyes, and listened to me preach as Pastor Preecha interpreted.

God's family is like a team. Some give of their finances. Some plant seeds of the Gospel. Some water. Some harvest. And God gives the increase. The excitement of being part of that team is like no other, though it may take tears, sweat and sacrifice. **Your gifts to missions also reap dividends you may never realize.** "They that sow in tears will reap in joy." (Psalm 126:5)

13

You Can't Make Up Stuff Like This!

As the ministry began to grow, many unexpected, almost unbelievable things blindsided us.

By the way, I don't think I explained where the name for our center, *The Vine Servicemen's Center*, originated. In the Bible Jesus said, "I am the vine, you are the branches." (John 15:5) The word *Vine* seemed to express the idea of something that was alive and growing. The handful of servicemen who began the work with us agreed it would be a fitting name for the new center.

Our ministry drew men and women from all backgrounds and denominations. About one third of our group was African American. Fortunately, we never had any strife among the various groups. One of my most able assistants was a tall dark Senior Master Sergeant Lou Harris - "Brother Lou." He was a God-sent man to us. I'll never forget a statement he made to our group as the time came for him to return to the States. He declared, "Men, we have learned to love each other. There is no difference in race as we are true brothers in Christ. And please don't forget this when you return to the States!"

JESUS AND JOHN THE BAPTIST ARGUE

One day I overheard a heated argument between two of our men. This was unusual, for we normally enjoyed great harmony. When I asked what the problem was, the answer blew me away. One man said he was John the Baptist while the other insisted he was Jesus. The most shocking thing about talking to "Jesus" was when I asked him where he was born. Without pausing for even a moment, he declared that he was born in Little Rock, Arkansas. I continued the chat just a few moments longer as it was getting pretty bizarre.

"Pardon me," I countered, "but I thought Jesus was born in Bethlehem, Israel."

"No," he snapped, "He was born in Little Rock!" I was speechless! What more could I say? Apparently one of us was crazy! Could it be that both men had been "shell shocked" by the Vietnam War?

At any rate, we were planning on a group outing with the men that day. I had chartered a 70-passenger bus to take us to the sapphire mines. The mines were about 80 miles away on the Thai-Cambodian border. However, I had to do something about these two guys fussing first. I soon had a most ingenious idea - I sat "Jesus" and "John the Baptist" side by side on the bus. Somewhere along the 3 hours journey their arguments ran out of steam.

Group Outing to the Sapphire Mines

Just an interesting sidenote: Once we arrived at the mines, several salesmen were hanging around urging tourists to buy what seemed to be beautifully cut and polished sapphire gems. I was tempted to buy one. Later as we watched a demonstration of the mining process, I realized the salesmen were selling fakes.

We observed genuine sapphires being mined by daring men who had dug deep holes into the ground with a shovel. With no supporting framework, the miners just climbed down into the holes and filled buckets full of tiny stones like gravel that they hoped would contain gems. The stones were then pulled up to the surface by assistants.

Up until that time, the only sapphires I had seen were the dazzling blue gems displayed in jewelry store windows. However, that day I realized they initially come out of the ground as tiny nondescript pebbles along with the gravel. The pebbles are then transformed by a tumbling and polishing process. An artist then completes the work by polishing and faceting them until they are totally transformed into something beautiful. IS THIS NOT A DESCRIPTION OF WHAT JESUS CAN DO IN OUR LIVES, IF WE LET HIM?

AMERICAN SERVICEMEN AS EVANGELISTS

The English classes at The Vine had now grown to an enrollment of about 100 students. Our GIs felt empowered as they taught. Never in their lives had they done so much to spread the Gospel to those in darkness. They reveled in the thrill of it. In their enthusiasm, they often left gospel leaflets on buses and around in public places. One young man, Jim Baggett who is now deceased, took a bus to Bangkok armed with a stack of tracks in the Thai language. At the main bus station, Jim walked around among the buses dropping leaflets on seats through the open windows. He had no idea where any of the buses were headed.

A few weeks later a missionary in Bangkok contacted us. Someone down on the Thai-Malaysian boarder, over 300 miles south, had written asking for information about a Bible course. The area from which the letter came was too perilous for missionaries or even the Thai military to travel. Communist separatists controlled the mountain villages. There were no churches or any knowledge of the Gospel in that pagan jungle area. Where had this man who lived in a danger zone gotten information about our mission's Bible correspondence courses? It turned out that he had picked up a tract Jim had left on a bus in Bangkok. Because of Jim, that man began to study the Bible. Furthermore, since Jim is now in heaven, the two have probably met.

On the Air Force base, the military officials were not at all thrilled about the tracts they found scattered around. On more than one occasion the head chaplain called me into his office to complain about leaflets with "The Vine" printed on the back cluttering up "his restrooms."

We always sought to build bridges to the chaplains on base. However, some of the chaplains saw our center as competition with their work, and resented us for it. One day we got an angry request from the head chaplain to come to his office immediately. When I arrived, he stood up to his full height, his eyes flashing and his demeanor one of authority and fury. He glared down at me and shouted, "One of your people just left my office. A local Thai police officer found him downtown where he had stripped off all his clothes. The cop brought him here to me. I asked the serviceman what he thought he was doing, and he told me he had just come from The Vine. What do you people at that place think you're doing? What kind of insane place are you running there?"

I had not the faintest idea who this serviceman was nor why this bizarre behavior. He was not one of our regular attenders at the Vine. One thing for sure, this chaplain already had thought all of us at the Vine were a bunch of kooks. This only reinforced his bias.

Certainly, this ministry was challenging as it grew, but the end results were more than worth it. You can't make up stuff like this.

14

Hero to Heel in 2 Hours

The Vine Servicemen's Center at Utapao, Thailand, became a place where American airmen could come and hang out after work, play games, listen to music, pray and talk over problems of the day. Sunday evenings we would all crowd around outside in front of our building before our regular service, broadcasting Gospel music and messages to the surrounding area. A church in the States had given us a powerful Bethany Broadcaster. This megaphone was a valuable tool for ministry. On Sunday evenings we prayed that the men headed up the highway for the bars might pass by, hear the music or messages, and stop. Possibly, they might even come into the meetings or just pause and think of where their lives were headed.

One night as we were outside about to enter our chapel, an agitated older American interrupted the gathering. In a drunken rant he shouted, "Why are you guys standing out here singing while a boy is dying?" By this time several curious neighbors had joined the crowd. Then we noticed a young Thai boy lying motionless on the ground at his feet. Obviously, the situation called for more than singing some songs. The agitated man began cursing all the phony Christians who could do nothing more than sing and hold their meetings.

I was caught off-guard. The young boy was lying there on the ground lifeless; he certainly needed a miracle. Our men spontaneously gathered around and cried out to the Lord for his recovery. The local Thais that gathered were all Buddhist. Buddhist prayers were usually chanted, and these people had never seen anyone cry out in desperation to a living God. In what seemed like a few moments, the lad began to stir and soon struggled to his feet. In awe and excitement, we all began to shout our thanks to the Lord. The half-drunk

American fellow gaped in astonishment, grabbed the child's hand, and staggered off into the darkness. In all the commotion I did not get their names, but this crowd of people would not have gathered unless we had had that Bethany Broadcaster. *That American church had no way of knowing how much their gift to missions meant to us.*

Most of our days in Thailand started rather routinely. One of the first and most important things to be done was to place our large water jugs in our van and head to the base for a fresh supply of safe drinking water. (That van, incidentally, had been donated to us by the Assemblies of God Youth of Tennessee.) The only water we could get otherwise, was muddy and contaminated. Local water came from a large tanker truck that had sucked up the water from ditches along the highway. Good water was essential for our family and for the airmen who would come to visit.

On one particular morning on the way to get water, I was shocked to see tanks and artillery guarding the front gate of the base. Normally, the security was rather relaxed. As I approached the check point, I sensed tension in the air. The gate guards seemed nervous as they checked my base pass thoroughly. I asked what was going on.

They abruptly shouted that the entire facility was about to go under immediate lockdown. If I entered the base I could not leave and if I left, I could not re-enter. In the years we had been in the area we had never experienced anything like this. On further inquiry, I learned the base had received word that a large contingent of Vietcong were heading our way. In the past there actually had been an event in which a communist Vietcong unit had penetrated base security. Their mission had been to blow up several of our B-52 bombers. Fortunately, they had been stopped before they could do any damage. For some time afterward, even those living off base were ill at ease.

The raiders on this day were reported to all be young men. The word was that they had commandeered three large orange highway buses as their cover. I quickly weighed my options. Time was of the essence. I turned the van around and rushed back to the center to warn our family. We closed and locked all the doors and windows, and our family hid under large tables. Then I thought of all the people in the area that had not received the warning. Most of those were families of the airmen on duty at the base. And none of the families had phones. (Cell phones were not yet been invented back then.)

Even though leaving the center seemed dangerous, I felt I had to do something. I ran back outside, jumped into the van, and gunned the motor. With the help of our Bethany broadcaster, I drove through our neighborhoods and surrounding areas warning everyone of a possible imminent Vietcong attack. When I returned to the family, I knew I had done all I could.

After hiding under our tables for another half hour, everything still remained quiet outside. No explosions. No warning alarms piercing the air. Once again, I climbed into our van and drove cautiously back towards the base. On reaching the entrance, I saw that the tanks and artillery were gone, and the guards were waving me through the front gates. I pulled one of the guards aside and asked him about the Vietcong attack. Oddly enough he began to laugh.

I did not see anything funny about the warnings we had received. He then explained that there had been an intelligence breakdown. The report that three busloads of Vietcong were coming to attack the base was based on a false rumor. Actually, three busloads of young Thai men *had* been headed our way, but it turns out they were Bangkok college students headed for a beach near the base. I was now double shocked. First, I had been alarmed by the warning and now shocked at how inaccurately the military had interpreted nothing but a rumor.

As quickly as possible, I returned to our home and told everyone they could get out from under the tables. Unfortunately, I had taken the broadcaster all around the area with a false report. Now I had to visit the same neighbors explaining I had made a mistake. In the space of two hours that day I had gone from feeling like a hero to feeling like a heel.

There must be a lesson to be learned from this embarrassing situation. I guess it demonstrates that a false report passed along by poorly informed people can wreak havoc in a neighborhood, among friends, in a family, and in a nation. Now, as social media flourishes in our country, misinformation can even spread unrest and uncertainty across an entire land.

James 3:5 "Likewise, the tongue is a small part of the body, but it makes great boasts. Consider what a great forest is set on fire by a small spark."

ALASKA

Dog sledding in the Far North, 1970.

KLANG, MALAYSIA

A new church begins with a "Good News Crusade" in a young pastor's living room.
(It eventually grew to become the largest gospel church in Malaysia.)

KENYA, AFRICA

Ministry in a rural school, 1968.

Staff Housing in a rural school in Kenya.

KENYA, AFRICA

Eating Posho and chicken with our fingers.

(Believe it or not, there's a real art to it. Not sure we got it right!)

ASIA

Children meet puppets, Jimmy and Bill the Bird.

As Gene preaches to adults and teens, Heather tells Bible stories and engages the children with Bible quizzes and games

(Sesame Street was not yet on TV, so kids and even adults flocked to see the puppets)

SEOUL, KOREA

School kids attend the evening children's rallies while Gene preaches to the adults and teens.

HONG KONG

Students attend school on the roofs of their apartments.
During our 6 weeks in Hong Kong, we visited different schools each morning,
Heather and her puppets shared the gospel with the children.

GUAM, 1970

An enthusiastic welcome by the Hippie "Jesus People" from one church.
We filled in for another missionary for 3 months in Guam. An exciting experience!

Scores of "Hippies" were saved and baptized in the Pacific Ocean in Guam.

GUAM

Gene preaching on the beach in Guam during a baptism.

BANGLADESH 1970

Gene learns to eat curry with his fingers in Bangladesh interior.
He had to reach the site by river boat. There were no roads.

ISTANBUL, TURKEY, 1972

During a stop-over in Istanbul on our way to Thailand, our little daughter
Deborah is fascinated with a bear performing on the street.

UTAPAO AIR FORCE BASE, THAILAND, 1972

"The Vine" recreation center and language school facility near the American base
began as place for GI's to spend their off-hours. As the men began teaching English
classes for local Thais, a new Thai church developed, and remains there today.

At "THE VINE," UTAPAO, THAILAND

American servicemen teach English to Thai students, using Bible Story books as texts.

Worship service at "The Vine" servicemen's center.

The iceman's daily delivery supplied our only source of refrigeration during our first days at "The Vine".

Servicemen head out on a field trip to the sapphire mines in Thailand.

UTAPAO, THAILAND

Behind "The Vine," just 30 feet from our home, prostitutes lured American men to their huts. Notice, they're built up on stilts.

UTAPAO, THAILAND, 1973

Our family gets around the area on a colorful baht bus. One ride costs 5 cents (one Thai baht)

A second new van, thanks to the Assemblies of God Youth of Tennessee!
This second van helped us transport American servicemen from the
base to our center, as well as taking men on field trips.

GULF OF SIAM, THAILAND

Baptizing the first converts who came to Christ through the language school.
(Pastor Preecha is the man wearing a tie)

PATTAYA, THAILAND

Church designed and built by Pastor Preecha, a former Buddhist monk. Young converts from "The Vine" moved to Pattaya, starting this new church.

GULF OF SIAM, THAILAND

Fishermen pulling brightly painted fishing boats to shore.

BANGKOK, THAILAND

Buddhist Stupa covered in gold leaf.

Our son, Som, pats a live Thai elephant.

A work elephant behind our "Speed-the-Light" car, is headed down a busy Bangkok street toward his next job-probably clearing land for a new building.

BANGKOK FLOODS

During the annual rainy season, people navigate Bangkok streets in boats.

BANGKOK FLOODS, 1978.

Boys use a raft to help get our car out of an apartment parking lot, Then guided
our car to the main street. Fortunately, the motor did not die.

BANGKOK STREETS, THAILAND

The royal palace.

THE FLOATING MARKET, BANGKOK

The Chao Phraya River flows through Bangkok much like a canal. Sales people sell wares from boats to customers who row their crafts along the waterway.

Breakfast for a Thai priest – each morning, Buddhist followers offer food to priests who walk past their homes.

Family noodle fest at an outdoor café.

THE PHILIPPINE ISLANDS

Water buffalo are the "tractors of Asia."
They plow the fields and help harvest the crops.

The quickest way to get a coconut.

RURAL PHILIPPINES, 1968

Beginning of a 7-hour trip on gravel roads on a local bus.

PHILIPPINES

Open air crusade

ANGELES CITY, PHILIPPINES, 1978

Deborah and Som with our dog Lucky, who was almost barbequed for a local feast.

MINDANAO, THE SOUTHERNMOST ISLAND OF THE PHILIPPINES

Our family visits a fishing village built on stilts, as civil war spreads across the island.
Som is sitting in the outrigger as Deborah makes new friends.

ANGELES CITY, PHILIPPINES, 1978

Heather's parents, Frank and Lillian Reed visit our family. Mr. Reed, an architect, offered valuable
advice in planning our new church building. Behind them is a nipa style play house.

ANGELES CITY, 1978

Our new church outside Clark Air Force Base.

Interior of our new fan-shaped church auditorium.

CLARK AIR FORCE BASE

This young motor-bike cop was also captain of the cross-country dirt bike team
The Lord turned his life around at Clark Church!

MOSCOW, RUSSIA, 1995

Sharing the Word of God through an interpreter in a Moscow public school.

MOSCOW, RUSSIA

Distributing Bibles in a public school in Russia.

A Russian Orthodox Cathedral open to the public – 25 years earlier only 1 church
In Moscow allowed public worship under the communist regime.

MONGOLIA

Mongolian gehrs (sheepskin igloos) serve as dorms for Bible school students

Gene stands beside a Mongolian Buddhist Urn.

Mongolian horsemen

BARTLETT FIRST ASSEMBLY, RENAMED "LEGACY CHURCH, BARTLETT"

In 1999 when Bartlett First Assembly of God searched for a new pastor, I was the only applicant. Later, we dedicated this lovely additional facility. Pastoring this church was one of the highlights of my ministry. I retired in 2014 on my 75th birthday, leaving the leadership in the capable hands of Pastor Johnny Byrd.

15

·◆·◆·◆·◆·

No, He is Not Drunk!

If you have been reading much of the narrative in this book, you might understand why I was under a great deal of stress 24/7 during our time in servicemen's work in Thailand. One night, the chapel service at our center had just begun. I stood before the men to say something. That's all I remember. According to Heather, it was 45 minutes later when I regained consciousness in the emergency room at the base hospital at Utapao. The doctor asked Heather if I was drunk.

She was horrified and declared, "Of course not! He's a minister!"

The doctor shot back, "What does that have to do with it?"

After examining me and running tests, the doctor concluded I was suffering from acute hypoglycemia, which is extremely low blood sugar - the opposite of diabetes. In some cases, this can be life-threatening. Normally, the base hospital does not treat civilians. But since airmen from the center had brought me in, I was reluctantly admitted to the base medical facility.

Most of that evening is kind of foggy in my mind. The only place in the hospital available for me was a bunk in a large ward with a number of other men. Unfortunately for me, my bunk was right beside the door to the psych ward. Sometime during the night one of the mental patients wandered in and stole my glasses that had been sitting beside the bed. Why would someone steal my glasses? Well, when someone has a severe mental condition, a lot of things they do make no sense! The next morning, I awoke with a horrible headache. Everything was blurry without my glasses.

Further exams concluded that I would be stable enough to be dismissed the next day. Really, I don't remember either going to the hospital or returning home back to the center. I was so weak that I found it nearly impossible to get out of bed. The doctors had warned me to be very careful of my diet. Doctors prescribed a high protein diet for the condition, and recommended 5 small meals daily, and no sugar. They warned me that this would be a life-long condition with no cure!

Back home, I noticed Heather had put a large jar of peanut butter beside our bed. For the next few hours, I was afraid to try to get up without first gulping down a huge spoonful of it, to get all the protein possible.

Somehow, even though no off-base phones were available, Missionary Bruce Mumm back in Bangkok got a message about my condition. The next day, Bruce made the 3-hour drive from Bangkok, and arrived at my bedside! At times like this, you don't need a sermon, just a Godly friend by your side! Through this ordeal, and so many others, Heather was always there, praying and encouraging. (Sometimes when I talk to young people, they tell me about someone they are attracted to. I tell them, "**Long term, the most important thing in a relationship, is not someone's appearance, but in a crisis, CAN THAT PERSON PRAY?**")

I don't recall much of what Bruce said during his short visit, but his presence meant everything. So often people are afraid to contact someone going through a crisis because they don't know what to say. **I remind people, it's not so important what you say - just be there.**

I do remember Bruce telling me that I must leave and get a break. With a weak voice I protested, "I can't leave the Vine! They need me!" Obviously, that was absurd. At this point *I* was the one who needed help! Bruce insisted that we leave that evening. This meant a dangerous late-night drive, 3 hours back to the Mum's home in Bangkok. Without my glasses, the glare of oncoming traffic made my head pound.

After being on the road about an hour, Bruce suddenly slammed on his brakes! Just a few feet ahead of us a large tractor was chugging along towing a disc plow. It was pitch dark and the tractor had no tail lights. If we had not stopped in time, the sharp edges on the plow would have killed us all!

Bruce wanted to take Heather and me to a missionary guest house on the coast. However, my first need was to somehow get new prescription glasses sent from Memphis to Bangkok. Heather and Bruce worked together to contact my Memphis eye doctor and have him relay my prescription to an optometrist in Bangkok. It seemed like a longshot because the prescription was complicated, but in 2 days, I had my new glasses! In a matter of minutes after putting them on, my headache began to subside!

Soon we were on our way to the coastal town of Hua Hin. I had heard of this area, but had never been to that region. Unfortunately, this meant another 6-hour round-trip drive for Bruce. I was overwhelmed by his patience and generosity! Time and again the Lord has provided people/friends to come to our rescue.

In Hua Hin we stayed in a neat, rather modest guest home on the seashore. There were neither TVs nor radios. The main entertainment was watching the cats that belonged to our host chase tiny lizards, called geckos, each evening. Our host knocked the geckos off the wall with a broom and the cats pounced on them and gobbled them down. Yuk!

Other missionary guests who, like ourselves, were "burned-out," shared stories of their experiences as we sat around chatting and enjoying wonderful healthy meals. The fellowship with other missionaries was uplifting. Each day Heather and I enjoyed long walks along the beautiful white beach, almost deserted except for one or two wooden fishing boats tied up to poles in the sand. There were few other local people or houses around.

Many years later, we attended a missionary conference in that same area. By then, luxurious hotels had been built all along the beach. I kind of liked it better when the area had been "forsaken."

One day on our walks we met an extremely friendly young Thai man. He asked if we had ever been to Phang Na? He explained it was only about ½ hour by motorboat out in the bay and offered to take us. Since we had lots of time, we decided, "Why not visit this site?" Looking back, we realize we were taking a risk. He could have robbed us and dumped our bodies in the ocean!

The motor boat ride was an adventure! We passed an entire village built up on wooden stilts over the water. Children splashed and played around the bamboo houses, waving at us as we passed.

The closer we got to the area of Phang Na, we were in awe. Out in the bay ahead, were huge (about 30 feet high) limestone formations chiseled over the centuries by wind and tide. The motor boat circled in and out around scores of these formations. We pulled up on a white sand beach at the entrance to a huge cave. We still have photos of this most unique area. Once again, we were all alone. Not one other tourist had discovered this treasure. Later, we saw photos of a James Bond movie filmed in this exact location! More recently we have seen updated photos of Phang Na in tourist magazines. There were so many tourists you could barely see the white sand!

All too soon our much-needed break in Hua Hin was over. It was time to return to Utapao and our center, The Vine. We had been blessed with several fine military men who had a vision and passion for ministry to their fellow GIs. I had tried not to worry about the work while we were gone. This was the Lord's work. But in the back of my mind, I knew the finances were tight and required constant oversight.

Before we left for that 2-week break, I had had a brief chat with my key assistant, Brother Lou Harris. At that time, I had asked him to take charge of the ministry in our absence. I trusted him, and we had a great relationship together. The only disagreement I had ever had with Lou was about tithing. He did not believe it was Biblical. He believed that people should give as they "felt led," (whatever that meant).

On our return to The Vine, the regular Sunday evening service was in progress. Brother Lou was preaching. Can you guess his sermon topic for that evening? TITHING! I was shocked, as we had debated about this subject. Later, up in my office, I asked him what had changed his mind about tithing. He confessed that he had no idea of how much it cost to run the ministry. He related, "One day as I looked at the stack of our bills and opened my Bible, something 'hit me.' I recalled all the chats we had had about tithing. It was as if a light clicked on in my spirit. I suddenly realized that tithing was not *your plan*, but *God's plan* to finance His work." From that time on, Brother Lou was a strong supporter of tithing for the financial stability of God's work.

Thank the Lord, today I have no trace of hypoglycemia! I eat desserts every evening and drink far more cokes than I should. Once again, God healed me of a disease that was supposed to have been incurable. Also, it is inspiring to recognize that in times of need, God brought people to our side to see His work go forward.

As you read these stories, I hope that they will boost your faith in God's mighty power. And may the Lord use you to **"just be there!"**

16

Som: A Special Gift from God

A MOTHER'S STORY

A new baby! The happy flurry of showers and gifts from friends and relatives – all the excitement and all the anticipation surrounding a new birth – these were not for me. For me there was only fear. My baby was about to arrive in a foreign hospital - in a foreign country! I could barely speak a few words of the local language. When the time came, how would I communicate with doctors and nurses?

It was February of 1973 and we were living in a squalid little community of hastily thrown together shacks.

The U.S. Air Force had arrived in Thailand to fight in the Vietnam War. Across the highway from the base, we had rented a large two-story concrete block building to use as a servicemen's center for our American Air Force personnel. The unpainted wood structures around us were mostly brothels with a few noodle shops, nail salons, and wood carving shops among them.

Our center sat a few yards back from the country's major east-west highway. All day long motorcycles roared past our home, weaving in and out between trucks piled high with chickens, pigs or vegetables. Big orange buses belched clouds of black smoke every time the drivers switched gears as they chugged past. Along the shoulders of the highway closer to Bangkok the nation's capital, we might even glimpse a driver guiding his elephant along, from high up on his wooden perch on the elephant's back.

My due date was coming closer and my anxiety was building immensely as the hot season was just beginning. How could I bring our new baby into the world in this heat in a local hospital staffed by people with whom I couldn't even communicate? The nearest hospitals to us were in Bangkok - 100 miles and over 3 hours away. My concern was, when labor started could we get to a hospital in time? The whole prospect was terrifying!

Carl and Dorothy Young, Canadian missionary friends of ours who lived in Bangkok, offered to let me stay with them until the baby arrived. Near their home, Gene located an excellent hospital run by the Seventh Day Adventist Church. At least one doctor reportedly spoke English. About a week before the baby was due, Gene drove me to Bangkok to the Youngs to get me set up. Back home, he had briefly left our 3-year-old daughter Deborah in the care of Newee and Peah, two young ladies who helped us cook and manage the center. These girls had become almost like trusted family members. One of them, Peah, who became a committed Christian, later helped establish a fledgling Thai church in that area.

I enjoyed visiting with our friends the Youngs, but after the second week I felt I had been imposing on their hospitality too long. The baby showed no signs of being in a hurry to enter our world. Perhaps we should have the labor induced and get this over with. Gene agreed, and returned to take me to the hospital on the agreed date, which seemed like the best idea at the time. Of course, we had no idea what lay ahead.

The good news: the hospital proved to be clean, pleasant and well-equipped. The bad news: the one English-speaking doctor for whom we had paid extra to deliver the baby, had left town on vacation. The nurses placed a long-distance call to him, during which he instructed them to go ahead and set up the procedure to induce labor. He graciously agreed to cut his vacation short.

In the delivery room the nurses placed me on a bed and began giving me little white pills. Gene nervously sat beside me writing letters, rubbing my legs from time to time, fussing over me, and asking the nurses useless questions they couldn't understand.

I had given birth to my first child in Memphis using natural childbirth, and figured I could handle a similar procedure in Thailand. However, these labor-inducing tablets caused much stronger contractions than with natural childbirth. Then the impossible happened - the supply of pills ran out! By then I was in agony without any medication for pain, and Gene was franticly trying to ask questions in English. The nurses helplessly threw up their hands and bombarded him with information in Thai. The stress on me only increased the pain.

The nurses set up saline drip equipment beside the bed, hung a bag of fluid from It, and attached a tube from that to a vein in my wrist. Gene, being a pharmacist, nervously checked the label on the bag. Saline! No way could saline induce labor! He was furious. "Get a hold of that doctor!" he demanded. "Wherever he is, I need to speak to him. NOW!"

Somehow, a hospital staff member made phone contact with the doctor again, and handed the receiver to Gene. The doctor patiently explained to him that although the bag was labeled saline, the nurse had added the correct amount of solution to the saline to induce labor. He also suggested that Gene leave and return to the waiting room, which left him none too happy.

After 2 or 3 hours of excruciating pain, I asked in broken Thai for the doctor immediately. "Doctor by nohn," a nurse replied. ("The doctor is asleep.") Asleep! What was he doing asleep? I begged the nurse to call him.

"We've got a problem," the doctor said after arriving and examining me. "I'm afraid this baby wants to come feet first. We're going to have to give you a spinal." By that time, I didn't care what he did as long as he made the terrible pain go away.

As the hours ticked by, the doctor was able to gently maneuver the baby into a head-first position. Then we waited - for a couple of hours! I realized then why the surgeon had gone to sleep before arriving. Figuring it would be a long night, he had tried to catch some shuteye before having to complete the delivery. At the time, he had not realized this little fellow was trying to come feet first.

Meanwhile, what was going on with the nervous father? As with most expectant fathers, he was pacing the halls, biting his nails, and in this case, sweating in the tropical heat. Then he remembered we had paid for the only air-conditioned patient room in the hospital. He located it, walked in, and shut the door. Wearily, he sat down in a chair and twiddled his thumbs. He looked over at the bed. Hmm - no one was using it at the moment. Why not? Removing his shoes, he crawled under the covers and relaxed.

The next thing he knew, the door was thrown open and a nurse screamed in Thai, "There's a man in the bed!" He jumped out of bed as two or three nurses stood staring at him. Fortunately, the only clothes he had removed were his shoes. And there was Heather being wheeled in with the cutest little baby boy in her arms.

After he admired his son for a few minutes, it was time to officially register this newborn with a birth certificate and name. As he left the hospital to fill out the paperwork, he first excitedly slipped off to a jewelry store to buy me an exquisite ruby ring I had admired, in honor of the occasion. Rubies are mined in Thailand and therefore had special significance as a gift.

Gene's official name is Doyle Eugene Burgess, Jr. That day we named our son Doyle Eugene Burgess, the III. When the Youngs dropped by later they said, "So, this is little Som. "*Som*" is the Thai word for *"three,"* or *"third."* Among friends and family, that name has stuck with him ever since. He was so cute! He still is to this day, but he would not want me to say so.

AND THEN – HE WAS GONE!

Som was a quiet, contented little fellow. He was about 2 months old when I strapped him into his baby seat, hopped on a baht bus, and headed for some nearby shops to look for fabric. A baht bus is an elongated jeep, brightly painted, and at the time it cost one baht (5 cents) to ride. When we arrived at our destination, I hopped off the bus and we entered a narrow shop filled with bolts of all kinds of cloth. Still strapped into his baby seat, I set Som on the counter where he sat quietly looking around. I began to search through the fabrics. The shop was crowded, not with many customers but with ceiling-high stacks of cloth all jammed into the shop's narrow space. I pushed toward the back looking for the perfect fabric for my latest project – I forget now what it was. But when I squeezed back through the aisle to the front counter again, my baby was gone!

A few months earlier I might have panicked, but I had been in Thailand a long time now. I chuckled, stepped outside and peeked through the window of the beauty shop next door. Sure enough, a Thai grandmother was holding my baby, still in his carrier, and showing off this little American fellow to all the customers. There he was, surrounded by adoring females, laughing and admiring him. He was quietly smiling and enjoying the attention. These gentle loving people would never hurt a child. I knew he was perfectly safe.

A NARROW ESCAPE

On another occasion about 8 months later, Som was happily playing with his toys on the floor. He was now about 10 months old. His sister, Deborah, was energetic and excited about everything, reminding me of a little twinkling star – bright, beautiful and fun. In contrast,

Som was calm, contentedly playing with his toys or perhaps enjoying the attention of the military men who came to the center. But I wondered - what if something happened to one of them here so far from home - maybe an accident or life-threatening disease?

I had come across a Bible verse: 2 Timothy 1:12, *"I am persuaded that He (God) is able to keep that which I have committed unto Him until that day (the day He returns to Earth)."* Would I be angry if God took one of my children from me, I wondered? I read that verse over several times. As I wrestled with the question of how far I could trust God with either child, I finally came to a conclusion. I made up my mind to totally entrust my children to God. Even if He took one, I would thank Him for the months and years He had lent them to me to love and enjoy. In my prayer that day I entrusted them both totally to God.

Som was less than a year old at this time. He could crawl and scoot around, but was still not walking yet. As he played with some toys on the floor, I sat chatting with a tall athletic African American fellow named Norm. Norm had served his 4-year term in the military and returned to civilian life. He now made a living teaching martial arts to young Thai men, which did not pay much. Perhaps that's why he ate with us along with several other GI's almost every day.

I was sitting on a straw mat on the floor with my back to the door. The highway was about 20 yards behind me. Norm sat on a bench facing me, just chatting about life in Thailand and his family back in the States. Suddenly he bolted from the bench, tore through the screen door, and raced across the parking lot right onto the highway, dodging cars and buses. What in the world? Stunned, I watched as he snatched my baby from the yellow center line of the highway. He raced back with Som safely in his arms! Now that I think about it, neither of us had heard the screen door open. How could he have gotten through that door and crawled that far unnoticed in a matter of seconds? I believe God was dramatically reassuring me that He *would* keep what I had committed to Him - my children.

From that day until the day we left Thailand, Norm was welcome at our dinner table. As far as we know, he never returned to the States, but we will never forget him. And though my children have both been through difficult times over the years, I will never forget God's assurance that He will take care of them to the end!

17

✦✦✦✦✦

The Bomb was Misloaded

My first flight on a military aircraft was alarming. It was a cargo plane - pathetically dilapidated – looking like it was ready for the junkyard.

The Vietnam war effort seemed to impact the entire Thai nation because they were deeply involved in supporting the anti-communist war effort in Vietnam. The largest American base in Thailand, Utapao, was across the main highway from our center. On that base were 10,000 American personnel. Besides this base, there were 7 other major US air bases on the Thai-Laotian border. On most of these bases the Assemblies of God sponsored fellowship groups. Periodically, I was able to visit most of these groups. These bases were under constant threat from Vietnamese communist artillery attacks. As I boarded the cargo plane that day, I felt it was crucial that I visit these men, to encourage them.

On that first flight, there were no refreshments served of course. All I got was torment from the veteran crew who thought it was funny to terrorize a civilian. The safety briefing, so called, was calculated to scare novices like me. I was not told about the plane's safety features designed to keep us secure. Instead, before take-off the loadmaster gave his speech that sounded something like this: "When we crash (not if we crash,) the plane will normally break into 3 parts. At this point, usually in the area above your head will be a large hole, and will be the safest place for you to climb out. Leave all your stuff behind and get away from the aircraft as quickly as you can before it explodes!"

The aircraft was terribly noisy. It rattled and shook as we taxied down the runway for takeoff and there were no windows to look out of to see where we were heading. At one point, the engines got so loud I figured we had probably climbed several hundred feet.

When I was able to raise myself up and get a glance through the one window in the ceiling, what a surprise! We were still bouncing and shaking down the runway! After that I decided not to try looking outside any more.

Flying on a military aircraft was a privilege that was rarely granted to civilians. I had to be assigned a military rank in order to complete the official travel documents that would allow me to board the plane. Someone in charge volunteered, "I'll help you fill out your flight papers. What rank would you like us to assign you, and I'll write it in this blank here?"

I stared in confusion at such a question. Then someone else asked, "How does 'Lieutenant Colonel' sound?" I was speechless, as he chuckled and wrote, "Lieutenant Colonel" on the page. Incidentally, I wish I had kept a copy of that document! When I returned to the base at Utapao, a senior commander somehow heard about the assigned rank – a status that outranked his own. He went totally berserk and called me into his office for a "meeting." In a jealous rant, he dressed me down with every demeaning name he could think of. Looking back now, the whole scenario seems ridiculous. Sometimes I just shake my head and think, You can't make up stuff like this.

On that flight we made a circuit that covered each of the 7 bases in Thailand along the Laotian border. I was thrilled to know I would be assigned quarters for "Lieutenant Colonel." Can you believe - my room was no different than the barest minimum the rest of the lower ranking crew were assigned, except my room had a jug of cold water.

Most of those visits to the bases and my ministry to our men were very rewarding. Often, I would speak in the base chapel on Sunday mornings and sometimes Sunday nights. During the week I would have a relaxed fellowship time with our military guys and enjoyed opportunities for counseling and Bible study with them. Not only did those men face the terrors of being in easy target range of the communist guerilla's artillery, but letters from home often brought them additional stress. Many times, wives wrote of their frustration over the duties of raising the children and caring for their daily needs alone.

War history is often reported in the media in a clean and neat set of statistics. But history books and TV news reports don't tell the stories of the human suffering and dirt and destruction behind the data. For instance, back at our home, across from the air base at Utapao we frequently watched plane after plane return after discharging their loads of bombs over North Vietnam. With each mission, untold numbers - possibly even hundreds - of Viet Cong lost their lives. As the bombers landed back on the tarmac they were immediately refueled and reloaded with bombs, carefully put in place by the loaders. Unfortunately, sometimes routines do not go like clockwork.

During one of my visits to a base up on the Vietnam-Laotian border there was an accident. Inadvertently, one of the bombs that had been loaded onto a fighter fell off as the plane began taxiing down the runway. This was not a catastrophe since the bomb had not yet been fused. But it caused a furor. One of the key leaders of our fellowship group had been responsible for overseeing the turnaround procedures, getting the planes reloaded and back into the air on time for their next mission.

The military had exacting procedures for accidents like a misloaded bomb. Unfortunately, part the equipment normally used for reloading a bomb was not available. So, my buddy found a forklift, used it to pick up the bomb and reload it properly. All went well.

The mission got off on time and was successful, but the Base Commander was irate with my friend, who happened to be leader of our Assembly of God fellowship group. He was reprimanded for not following precise guidelines. As tempers flared, I was glad that I was there to support my Master Sergeant friend when this happened.

The Base Commander called for a court martial by the other senior military officers.

For some reason, it didn't seem to matter that my friend did the only thing he could do to reload the bomb. The most important thing the high-ranking brass was concerned about was he did not do it "according to the book." In spite of his taking quick action and the fact that there had been no damage, he was court-martialed, reprimanded, fined, reduced in rank and sent back to the States humiliated. At least I was there to put an arm around his shoulders and pray that God would give him grace for this terrible injustice. The ranking officers sometimes feel they have to show their power and authority regardless of who gets hurt – and that is sad.

WARTIME AIRCRAFT

Just across the highway from our center, "The Vine," was a military parking site for a variety of aircraft. I had always had an interest in all kinds of airplanes. At Utapao and most overseas military bases, military aircraft are not equipped with noise suppressors. The base operated 24/7 and the noise was so loud it constantly rattled our windows.

The most impressive plane was the gigantic **B-52 bomber**. Each bomber required 8 engines to get it airborne with its bomb load. One day our Assembly of God chaplain took me on what he called a "ministry of presence." He loaded the back of a pickup with ice and hundreds of cold Cokes. Then we drove along the normally restricted flight line just to chat with the airmen and pass out ice cold drinks. These visits were very welcome in the tropical heat of Thailand, and it was even hotter for the men working around the planes. The noses of some of our B-52's sported red stars. The chaplain explained that each red star indicated that the gunners on that plane had downed an enemy aircraft.

Each plane had unique protection features: flares that could be shot out from their wings to divert any heat-seeking missile that might be aimed at it. Along with flares, another compartment was filled with hundreds of little metal balls that could be disbursed into the air to confuse any radar-guided missiles.

The B-52 pilots were a cocky, arrogant bunch. Each day they were given briefings on their success at hitting their targets on the previous day. The bombers' missions were directed by GPS and specific coordinates. The pilots simply flew to the designated coordinates, punched a button, the bombs dropped, and the pilots returned to the base to celebrate. The planes flew so high the pilots rarely saw their targets until seeing them on film at the next day's briefing. The crews felt they were so macho and invulnerable that part of the so-called "briefings" had playboy photos mixed in with film of their last mission, and their instructions for the next operation.

The crews were encouraged to attend chapel, but rarely did. However, if something went wrong, they did somehow find the time to attend. All during their bombing runs over North Vietnam, ground-to-air missiles were constantly being fired at them. But none of the rockets could reach our high-altitude bombers. *But one night the Russians delivered their latest high-altitude rockets to North Vietnam.* They were called SAM-2's (surface-to-air missiles.)

I happened to be near the runway and observed the first of our bombers return to the base after having been struck by a SAM-2. The missile had damaged part of the plane's tail, including the guidance system. The bomber made it back to the vicinity of the base, but had little control for the actual landing. The giant bomber skidded along one side of the runway, through a fence, across the highway and into some woods. No one was killed but all the crew were injured. This put a scare into all of the crews because it was now clear they were no longer invulnerable. Who do you think found time to be in the chapel the next Sunday morning and many Sundays that followed? The air crews! Now each time the chaplain made a visit during the pilots' daily briefing, there was serious prayer!

OTHER WARTIME AIRCRAFT

Besides the B-52, there was the **KC-135 Tanker**, often called the "Flying Gas Tank." These tankers were designed to meet up with the fighters and bombers for mid-air refueling during their missions. While chatting with the pilots one day, some of the men who were "boom operators" on these tankers described to me their job. The boom is like a very long hose with something like a wing on its tip. The boom can be maneuvered to the nose of the plane needing fuel. The two planes have to get within just a few yards of each other to do the refueling. By this method, a fighter plane or a bomber can stay in the air indefinitely. (Maybe it's only guys, not women, who care about this stuff?)

The "**Blackbird**" was by far the most dramatic aircraft on the base. It was officially the **SRT-71**. It was painted black, and performed more like a missile with a pilot, than like a plane. It was super-secret and "did not exist" as far as the public was told. It would roll out to the runway and quickly take off like a rocket, fly straight up, and disappear. The pilots were equipped with the same gear as our astronauts, since the plane would operate at heights above 100,000 feet. Their main mission was reconnaissance. They could photograph enemy positions with cameras so accurate they could read a license plate even 100,000 feet above the earth. These planes were so fast they even outran enemy missiles.

Perhaps the most exotic aircraft was the now famous **U-2**. This was the plane shot down by Russia during the height of the cold-war. Back then, President Dwight Eisenhower declared that such a plane did not exist. In what was America's most embarrassing moment, the Russian Premier actually produced the flight gear and a photo of our captured pilot, Francis Gary Powers at the UN conference. It was never clear how his plane was shot down while flying at the edge of space.

Again, these U-2's were so secret that they were kept out of view and their existence was denied. The planes would take off and begin gradually climbing in wide circles, so that on take-off and landing they were quite visible. The distinctive thing about them was a very narrow fuselage and extremely long droopy wings. Their mission was aerial photography.

Often in the late afternoons these U-2's would fly low circles in the area of our center, looking like gliders. On landing, they were so visible it was hard to deny their existence!

Today, up-dated versions of most of these aircraft are still flying. With our amazing American technology, we wonder if today new experimental aircraft are out there – aircraft that we know nothing about? That is certainly possible!

18

Ordered to Close the Thai Orphanage

I had received orders from my superiors to close our orphanage in Thailand. Why, I wondered?

Reaching out to the local Thai people, urging them to turn from idols to Christ, was part of our ministry and that of our men. We saw many of them give their lives to the Lord. While visiting the seven bases along the Thai-Laotian border, I always encouraged our military men to reach out to their buddies as well as to the Thai community. It was a delight to visit the bases and see our American fellows worship side-by-side with their Thai brothers who were new converts.

I did have one very disturbing assignment on a specific trip to one base along the Thai-Laotian border. My accommodations there sat right beside the runway. The constant roar of fighter aircraft beside my tiny room was jarring. It is hard to describe the deafening noise from those powerful jet engines just a few feet away.

However, this was not the most difficult thing about my trip. The most difficult thing - I was assigned to tell the men on that one base to close their orphanage! Our men there were so excited about their ministry to Thai children. Their excitement was contagious. It was great just being around these men. Unfortunately, this made my visit and assignment that much more difficult.

The military leaders on the base were quite happy with all that the men were doing for these orphans and local children living in poverty. But word got back to my superiors in the U.S. and they were upset. Technically, the group of men who had started the orphanage was supposed to have had an official letter filed with our head office back in the States. Not knowing about this requirement, the men had carried out the ministry in the best way they knew. A Thai church in the area was helping to staff and oversee the effort.

My superiors in the regional Missions office were not particularly impressed with the orphanage, despite the lives that were being salvaged. To be fair, no official missionary had been assigned to oversee the project, or to manage and fund it after the Americans left. The officials were disturbed because it had not been approved by them and had not gone through the proper channels. As in the case of the bomb being dropped on the runway, this was another case of things not being done "by the book." I really was not sure if the concerns of some leaders were about the protocol and regulations not being followed, or was it more about their personal authority being violated?

My specific assignment in visiting this base was to tell the airmen that they must close the off-base center they had started, as well as the orphanage. Well, to someone sitting at a desk many thousands of miles from the site, the orders being given might seem easy to follow: "Just do what you're told."

In some ways this was not an orphanage in the truest sense of the word. It was more like a daycare. It was also a place for fellowship and Bible teaching where many of the local parents and adults gathered. Some of the children who attended had fathers who had been drafted into the Thai military during the Vietnam conflict. Thus, a wide variety of people continually met together at the facility, along with the children. But the main goal of the servicemen was to bring as many as possible from this community to Jesus.

The bottom line was, I had been given a specific assignment to make the long journey up to the border to tell those in charge that they had to close their center and send the children back to their villages. As I journeyed north toward the base that day, I kept wondering how I would break this terribly difficult news.

On my arrival, the men welcomed me warmly. I had several days of wonderful fellowship with these men, the orphanage staff, and some of the children. Yet my stomach got tighter and tighter with each passing day. I put off telling them the terrible news as long as possible. Finally, I called the leaders and even the children together to pray with them. They had no idea why I had come and what I had been commissioned to do.

As I looked into their faces, it seemed almost criminal for me to close a center that was doing so much good, regardless of what the rulebook said. Instead of closing the center at that meeting, I did what I felt was pleasing to the Lord. I simply prayed for God's blessing on them and silently prayed that my superiors back home would understand.

Unfortunately for me, they did *not* understand. I was severely reprimanded for not following the directions of those in charge. This "insubordination" tended to paint me as a rebel in the eyes of some of my superiors from then on. But we had *been* there, "where few had dared (or cared) to go," and we did what we felt the Lord had directed us to do. I have never regretted that decision.

19

The Forgotten War

Warning: these facts are extremely disturbing.

For many of us, Vietnam is a far-off place. But to those Americans who fought in the Vietnam war, it's a constant and painful memory. It was because of this war that America had many troops based in nearby Thailand. We felt there was a desperate spiritual need among them, and for this reason we established a servicemen's center for our troops there in Thailand. Many thousands of American servicemen today still suffer from Post-Traumatic Stress Syndrome as a result of that conflict. The defoliate, Agent Orange, that was used on the jungle growth has been linked to a variety of cancers suffered by veterans of that war. The chemical would be similar, but more powerful than the "Round-Up" that many Americans use in our yards. We can see several parallels between that Asian conflict and the war in Afghanistan.

BACKGROUND HISTORY

During World War II, the Japanese had conquered most of Southeast Asia. They were ruthless rulers. But when Japan finally lost that war, the French moved into Vietnam, Cambodia and Laos. These nations, fed up with being under the rule of conquering powers began to resist, keeping the French invaders in constant turmoil. The Vietnamese were poorly armed, while the French had the latest military equipment. However, the Vietnamese army in the north gained more and more influence. Then Communist China began to supply equipment and men to the Vietnamese.

It was not long until the French troops were in constant retreat. Finally, the French troops retreated to a mountainous region of, DIEN BEN PHU. The French troops faced heavy bombardment for 2 months. Their men were killed by the hundreds. Their only option was a humiliating surrender to the Vietnamese in 1954.

Thus began the long retreat for the defeated French. Eight thousand of the surviving French soldiers were marched 500 miles northward. Sadly, one half died on the horrific trek as the French power in Southeast Asia ended.

Were there any lessons to be learned from the French defeat? General Dwight David Eisenhower, a hero of World War II, had some valuable advice to give America. He was a student of warfare and had master-minded the landing at Normandy, rescuing France from Nazi Germany. His advice was, "NEVER GET INVOLVED IN A GROUND WAR IN SOUTHEAST ASIA." Maybe we should have listened to him!

THE COST OF WAR

If you examine the vast numbers of our men critically injured during the Vietnam War, and consider the hundreds more men that were killed, the war was a terrible tragedy. At least 2 million local civilians died, plus 400,000 boat people died fleeing the country. Besides these, 60,000 American troops lost their lives, along with 2.6 million South Vietnamese troops, and 1.1 million North Vietnamese and Viet Cong. If you realize the millions of dollars what were spent on the war rather than on badly needed projects at home, you begin to get an idea of how bitter the waste of that war was!

One day while filling in for a pastor in Guam in the early 1970's, I visited the military hospital on that Pacific island. Most of the wounded were about 25 to 30 years old. Some had been brought to the facility, first by jet airlift, and then transferred on what was called a stretcher bus to the hospital. Some had been rushed to the facility so quickly they were still partially covered in dirt from the battlefield in Vietnam.

Visits to the military hospital became more sobering each time I went. On one visit I stopped by some beds, (and there were scores), just to try to comfort the men. One fine looking young man had multiple injuries. Both of his legs had been blown off at his waist.

The doctors had administered such heavy doses of morphine, he had no realization that he had lost his legs. I wish I could say this was the only case in which I saw such horrible injuries. There were numbers of others who had indescribable wounds. And all had long-lasting emotional wounds.

MANY HISTORIANS ASK, "WHO REALLY WON THE VIETNAM WAR?"

When the French were forced out of what was called Indo-China (Laos, Cambodia and Vietnam), the USA was afraid that the Communists would take advantage of the vacuum. The basic premise of all the trouble was FEAR OF WHAT THE OTHER SIDE WOULD DO! American patrol boats cruised near the coast of Vietnam, keeping watch.

It was not long until tensions boiled over between the US and the heavily communist-influenced nation of Vietnam. One of our patrol boats off the coast was supposedly fired on by the communist forces. The USA felt they could be facing a serious escalation of communist hostilities. The response was to send a small number of American troops to the country. The communists felt this was a threat. They increased their military strength. With their increased strength, the USA felt we should match the communist build-up. Any increase by one side was met with an equal increase by the other side. It is hard to believe this went on, back and forth, for about 20 years.

The US commanders continually pushed for "just 10,000 more troops and we could win." And this number was continually increased. By 1968 we had 549,000 troops in Vietnam and 50,000 in neighboring Thailand. Added to this were the many thousands of support troops in Japan and South Korea. In 1968 alone we spent 569 billion dollars on the war effort. Unfortunately, we had nothing to show for all that we expended in men and materials. Untold numbers of our men suffered from the effects of Agent Orange. Thousands of gallons of it were sprayed from our planes to destroy the jungle canopy between North and South Vietnam. Beneath the canopy were hidden vast amounts of weaponry smuggled south by the communists. Even by changing our commanders on the ground, or by dropping more bombs, or adding thousands more of our young men, nothing stopped the steady North Vietnamese gains.

Unfortunately, the South Vietnamese commanders all seemed to be corrupt. None of them really had the support of their people. It seemed that the leaders were happy to **let the USA fight their war!**

The South Vietnamese gradually retreated toward their capitol in Saigon. They had lost the will to fight and our men were dying daily. Finally, in what was called the TET OFFENSIVE, the Communists overwhelmed Saigon. Our humiliated American troops were hastily withdrawn to nearby ships. Those Vietnamese troops that had been loyal to the US were captured and treated horribly. This was the first war the USA ever lost! **Unfortunately, the confusion created by our hasty withdrawal from Vietnam parallels our recent withdrawal from Afghanistan.**

TODAY

In 2021 as we look back, we realize many of our fears were not realized. As stated earlier, it was fear that the North Vietnamese would invade the neighboring countries and spread communism, that triggered American participation in the war. Even though both Russia and China were deeply involved, it was **FEAR THAT IGNITED THE VIETNAM WAR**. The communist government of China had allied with the North Vietnamese, but China was not able to control them when the war was over. Now we can we see that many of our fears were unfounded. While the Vietnamese adopted communism, they did not invade their neighbors! **And so the answer to the question many have asked: Who won the Vietnam war? The answer: NO ONE WON THE VIETNAM WAR!**

OUR ALLIES

It is hard to realize that the Vietnamese as a nation would not forever hate us and be our enemies for generations. Yet, today we have a good relationship with them - with their government and the local people. We have solid trade relations, and our ships refuel in the ports we once bombed!

UKRAINE

3/08/2022. At the time of this writing, Russian Leader Vladimir Putin has sent troops along with their jet fighters, cruise missiles, tanks, etc. to invade neighboring Ukraine. The Ukrainians have had little but small arms with which to fight back. Hundreds of thousands of Ukrainian lives will be lost, along with untold numbers of Russians. At the time of this writing, over half a million Ukrainians have fled to neighboring countries. Many Ukrainian towns and cities have been reduced to piles of rubble. Who is really winning this war? There seems to be no way a peaceful Ukraine can survive this onslaught.

We are forced, in the light of history, to ask if there is another way - a better way to solve our differences without war? The Bible speaks of a coming day, "**They will beat their swords into plowshares and their spears into pruning hooks. Nation will not take up sword against nation. NOR WILL THEY TRAIN FOR WAR ANYMORE!** (Isaiah 2:4) Only when Jesus, the Prince of Peace, returns will we then have peace and safety.

20

✦✦✦✦

Invitation to the Big Time

WHERE DO WE GO FROM HERE:
MALAYSIA, INDONESIA, SINGAPORE, HONG KONG?

As the Vietnam war was winding down, the number of troops at Utapao was reduced drastically, and we knew that the base would soon close. It was time to go home for a year of travel, visiting churches to thank them for their past support, and raising money for the next assignment.

The big question was: Where was the next assignment? Our hearts were in Thailand with the Thai people. Bangkok seemed to be a logical place to return, but trying to learn the Thai language was about to drive me nuts! It is a tonal language, and I just couldn't get the tones right.

Our Missions Department was aware of the problem I had with the Thai language. They were also aware that we had traveled much of the world in ministry and were familiar with a variety of cultures. They suggested several alternate places of ministry. The Assemblies of God has a correspondence school (Global University) with branches all over the world. At that point it was called ICI (International Correspondence Institute.) The Missions Department suggested we visit Malaysia and think about leading ICI there. I had preached in Malaysia many times in churches and conducted seminars etc. Before returning to the States we made a trip to Malaysia to investigate the need there.

Some of the leaders were dear friends that urged us to return after our furlough and work with them. The capital city of Kuala Lumpur was modern, clean, efficient, prosperous, and safe. I had known the general superintendent in Malaysia, Prince Guneratnam, since he was a Bible school student and I would like to have teamed up with him.

As I observed the situation, I explained to Superintendent Prince that the ICI outreach was doing exceedingly well already. In fact, all the Malaysian ministries were very well organized. In the natural, this would be a pleasant place to work, especially after some of the struggles we had had in Thailand. It would have been easy to make a decision to accept their invitation, except there was no "OK" from God.

We were also offered an open door in Indonesia where we had ministered several times. Again, I felt this was not the place for us. Finally, I wondered if our missionary leaders were getting disgusted with my indecision. Their last suggestion was, "Why don't you locate in Singapore or Hong Kong? There are so many travel connections out of those cities. From there you could travel and minister easily almost any place in Southeast Asia." We were highly honored by these suggestions.

Again, we were well acquainted with our leaders in those two cities and had ministered in both. However, I would need to use interpreters in many of those Asian countries. After preaching through interpreters for so many years, I realized I was actually preaching to the interpreters, and they were the ones preaching to the people. At times they would confuse the messages. I might be talking about "spiritual warfare," and they would be speaking to the people about "welfare."

But neither Heather nor I felt at peace about any of these choices. Thus, we decided we would return to Bangkok and do everything we could to strengthen the work among the Thai people.

As we prepared to leave Thailand for furlough in the States, I noticed a letter that I had overlooked a few days earlier. It was from Brussels, Belgium. But who would be writing from Brussels, and how would they know where we were? The letter was from one of the most respected leaders in our Assemblies of God fellowship. The opening of his letter was a shocker! "Gene, this is God! You need to relocate to Brussels, Belgium as soon as possible!" Due to other missionaries' furloughs, he felt we were the ideal people to give temporary leadership in any one of a variety of ministries in Brussels in their absence.

You cannot take everyone seriously who claims to hear from God. But this gentleman was a "giant in the faith!" The position in Brussels was a PLUM-the most influential in Central Europe. We really did pray. This would be a great clean, centrally located place to live. And there was a teaching position open in our school. THE CONTINENTAL BIBLE SEMINARY. In the natural, I wanted to get out of the garbage piles of Utapau and move to Brussels, a world-class city. But in my heart, I knew that this was not God's will.

SOMETIMES SINCERE PEOPLE THINK THEY KNOW WHAT GOD'S WILL IS FOR US!! Some people even want someone to tell them what God's will is for them. But this type of advice can lead to error and disillusionment. Not every open door is a door God has opened. When seeking God's will in a situation, after you pray and do all you can, just recognize that *in God's will, there is peace, even in times of indecision.*

We left Thailand for home, still unsure of our next assignment. "Home" was Memphis, Tennessee. By now we had two small children, ages 1 and 4. Heather watched the children while I travelled the country for a year. I visited churches that had supported us, and raised money for our next overseas assignment.

As I travelled, another invitation came to us. Our missionary pastor at Clark Assembly of God in the Philippines (a servicemen's church) was retiring. The church was across the street from Clark Air Force Base, the largest American base in Southeast Asia. After that period of indecision, we felt God leading us to this open door. At last we felt peace. *This* was where God wanted us.

21

The $5,000 Cake – Manila, Philippines

This experience is one of the most unusual I have ever encountered. I have never written about these events nor told anyone outside my family, yet since this happened so many years ago, it can be told now.

As the Vietnam war was coming to a close, many of the American GI's were reassigned from Thailand to the Philippines. We continued our ministry to the military by accepting an invitation to pastor a church outside Clark Air Force Base in the Philippines.

Every year the Assemblies of God missionaries in the Philippines gathered for a special conference in Manila where we had fellowship, inspiration, and discussed plans for future ministry. One year the conference took a bewildering twist. We were late arriving at the business session that afternoon, but no worries, it was usually boring anyway. We had driven about 70 miles from our church in Angeles City, to the conference which was being held in a Manila hotel. In the meantime we were in the middle of exciting plans to build a new larger auditorium at our own church. We needed to accommodate the growing number of U.S. military families and some local Filipinos who were now attending.

As we entered the hotel conference room in Manila, the annual financial report on our various missionary projects was being discussed. Yet an unusual sense of tension seemed to pervade the room. Apparently, the tension related to the financial report. This part of the meeting was typically time-consuming and mundane. When someone handed us a copy of the report as we found a seat, we were shocked! The report revealed that several thousands of dollars were missing from our National Missions Account in the Philippines.

Further, funds for our own building project outside Clark Air Force Base were included in the missing funds.

HOLD ON! We will get to the chocolate cake in just a minute.

As I read the report, chills ran down my spine- - $5,000 for our church building project had been misappropriated! I did not believe any of the money in the account was stolen. Our business manager was a good Christian and a personal friend, but he had made some bad decisions. I was obviously quite disturbed. How could I stand in front of our congregation back at Clark and report that much of the money they had given was missing?

What had happened was that our Field Treasurer, "Jim" had placed almost all of the mission's money in what was supposed to have been a high-yield investment account. He had done this without anyone's approval. Unfortunately, the local businessmen who received this money from him turned out to be dishonest. I was quite upset because I was ultimately responsible for $5,000 of these funds for our new building. We had worked hard raising this money and many of the people in the church had given sacrificially. While on furlough, we had asked churches back in America to help in this project. One of our young Filipina ladies had even placed her solid gold necklace on the altar. The value of the chain was equal to about a year and a half of her wages. How could I tell the church members their money was gone?

I turned to Heather and whispered that something had to be done and done quickly. There had to be a way of recovering at least part of this money. I silently sought the Lord for some answer. I told Heather, "I'm going to leave, search for a bakery, and I will try to buy the biggest chocolate cake available."

While the meeting was in an uproar, I quietly stepped away, and drove through Central Manila. My plan was to find an open bakery and purchase the biggest chocolate cake possible. The next step then was to find the area treasurer who was holding all our money for "safekeeping," if any of it was left. Next, in my mind I tried to develop a strategy for getting our money back.

I drove through the hectic evening traffic and found an open bakery where I purchased the largest chocolate cake they had. Afterwards I searched for Jim's home in suburban Manila. I figured he would be there, because he certainly had not been at the meeting. Since Jim would be called on to give a full accounting of the missing money, he had a good reason not to show up at our annual gathering. Frankly, I was quite distressed about confronting him. Jim was a good friend of mine, and many in our church were fond of him. I do not think Jim actually stole any money, but had placed much of it in the hands of dishonest people. Yet, I suspected he still had control of a great deal of our building funds. Prayerfully, I approached Jim's front door. I knocked a few moments and nobody answered. I knew that Jim was there along with his family. A few more knocks finally brought him to the door.

I handed him the cake, and he invited me in. I told him that I had a problem. I confronted him about our church's missing money. At first, Jim said he knew nothing about the missing funds. Then he assured me he could not locate any money that might be missing at that late hour. However, I suspected that he might have stashed some of it in his house. That's when I told him that I would sit with him until the money appeared, even if it took all night. After a short while he decided to "search" for our money. It wasn't too long until $5,000 miraculously appeared. He thanked me for the cake and quickly ushered me out the door. I hid the money securely in the trunk of our car and hurriedly returned to the hotel where the meeting was still in progress. This is how we were *"saved"* by a $5,000 cake!

What we did not know and should have been told was that Jim had played a role in a similar experience in another mission field where he had been the treasurer. He had placed the mission's money in the hands of a "great businessman." Sad to say, there had been some funds missing there also. There is a great lesson to be learned here: even good people should never be given the sole responsibility for handling someone else's money without proper checks and balances governing its use and distribution.

This was just the beginning of the many challenges that lay ahead as we began a very ambitious building project in a third world country. **Unknowingly, we were venturing where few had dared to go.**

22

Construction Chaos Drives
Pastor Berserk

SEARCING FOR AN EXPERT ARCHITECT

With God's help, we had retrieved the $5,000 missing from our building account. The small church in which we had been meeting needed to be replaced with a larger building, and we now had the initial funds to start work on that dream. We had no idea that retrieving those funds was only the beginning of an arduous 2-year uphill struggle that lay ahead. Every building project involves challenges, but they increase ten-fold in a third world country.

Angeles City had grown up around Clark Air Force Base on the Island of Luzon, Philippines. Concrete walls surrounded the houses on the town's streets. On the tops of the gray walls, broken glass embedded in concrete kept thieves at bay. Most families, ours included, kept guard dogs to further protect their property. Angeles City was the place we had agreed to settle for four years to pastor the church and minister to the American servicemen stationed there.

Theft was a problem, but basically this was a slow-paced island society of friendly, family-oriented folks traditionally involved in agriculture or handcraft manufacturing. In those days there was very little industry beyond small family businesses. Many people lived at a bare subsistence level, sharing what little they had with friends and family members in need.

Caring for each other and sharing was an expected and ingrained part of life that we as Americans did not fully understand. For example, one day the German Shepherd dog that protected our home and possessions went missing. He was a pretty fierce dog and took his duty of protecting the family and property very seriously. But he had disappeared. Perhaps one of us had left the gate open.

A couple of mornings later, a Filipino friend arrived at our house bringing "Lucky" back home. Our friend had rescued him from a barrio (small village) where he had been caged until it was time for a fiesta, at which time he was due to be barbequed. Apparently, no one in the barrio had a pig to roast, so they had "borrowed" our dog. They must have drugged him first, or he would have torn any intruder to pieces. Obviously, the line between theft and borrowing was fairly ambiguous in that society.

Maybe we should have bought a pig for families in the barrio, to replace the dog. After all, we were rich in their eyes and could easily have provided food for their celebration. Such cultural differences between American life and island living constantly blindsided us during those days. As we reflect back on those experiences now, we laugh at the confusions we constantly encountered during those four years.

The Philippines is a Catholic country. Architects have erected magnificent rectangular-shaped cathedrals throughout the islands; however, we wanted a fan-shaped interior. As we searched for a professional architect, we began to realize none of those men we spoke to had ever seen a fan-shaped auditorium. We felt the curved shape would give the attendees a better view of both the platform and each other, thus increasing a sense of unity among the people.

Some potential architects scratched their heads and sketched out circular sanctuaries with a baptismal pool in the center, while most simply could not grasp the concept we had in mind. We finally found a woman architect who had designed a church for another mission in Manila and was willing to work with us. She drew up the plans and we hired her as both architect and contractor.

Right away, our new architect hired a team of workers to begin constructing the church foundation. They began excavating in order to locate solid rock on which to lay the footings. They worked with hand shovels, while wiping the sweat from their brows and muttering to each other in Tagalog. All day long they worked, piling up heaps of sand without finding rock. If they continued, I feared they might find themselves in China as we watched the mountains of sand grow.

About that time, my father-in-law, Frank Reed and his wife Lillian, arrived from Canada to visit us for a few days. Mr. Reed, an experienced architect, walked around the site that first day of their visit, his 6-foot frame towering over the shorter workmen as they looked up at him in frustration. With a deep sigh he surveyed the useless holes they had dug, rubbed a hand over his bald head, and advised the architect. "Let's go inside,"

Around the dining room table he explained to us that the ground in this area was primarily composed of sand with no rock on which to build. However, all was not lost. "We can make our own artificial foundation in the sand," Sketching on a notepad he explained, "We can fill these existing holes with first-class cement. When it is still semi-solid, the steel reinforcement rods can be hammered down into the cement and the concrete slab foundation laid on top."

I don't know what we would have done unless Heather's dad had decided to visit us. He was a tremendous help in many other ways as well. As always, God's plans and timing are perfect!

With one challenge behind us, we knew there would be more. Just a few days later the contractor/architect met with me and confessed she was unqualified to select the proper structural engineer for the building.

Why had she not told us this at the onset? I was a pharmacist, not a builder. I could count pills but I sure was not qualified to select a structural steel engineer. In this entire region there were few people qualified to build more than a house, office or a traditional church. The architect said, "Pastor Burgess *you* will have to choose the man who can do the complex steel work." I was stunned to realize the incompetence of the people on which I had to depend. I stood there speechless as she handed me briefs of the "experts" I could interview.

Many nights after that I sat alone in my office praying and scanning plans I did not understand. I was crying out to God for some kind of divine revelation and guidance. I did not have the faintest idea of how to go forward. As I sought the Lord, I felt He gave me a rather simple idea. The idea involved interviewing each of the prospective engineers and praying the Lord would give me insight to ask the right questions, and then grant me the discernment to know who was most qualified. I felt I was swimming in deep water and a mistake in judgment could mean a faulty building and a great waste of money. Don't you wish you could have been there to help me figure this out?

On several nights two of our most committed board members drove by the church office and saw the lights on. They knew that something unusual was going on at 2 o'clock in the morning. These men, still in their fatigues, had been at work on the flight line across the street at Clark Air Base. Lloyd Francis who is now an ordained minister and missionary to the Philippines was one of those men.

The second man, John Birkinbine, was a top-quality man who was always willing to do whatever he could to help anybody. Unfortunately, after he had been discharged from the Airforce for just a few months, he was helping a friend do some heavy automotive work. That day there was an accident, and John slipped away into the arms of Jesus. I will never forget those men who dropped by so many nights and simply laid their hands on my shoulder letting me know they were with me 100 percent. I could not share with these younger men some of the complex things I was trying to handle at the time, yet they stood with me during this challenging time.

The next thing we had to do was hire an electrical engineer for some very heavy-duty complex wiring for the massive central air-conditioning system. Once again, the architect came to me and said, "Pastor, I am not qualified to make this decision." It seemed the load got heavier and heavier as I had no one with real ability to help us. These challenges happened repeatedly as we searched for qualified people with which to work.

Another unexpected cultural challenge we experienced involved the workers bringing their families to live with them on the job site. This was a surprising but common practice with construction crews in the region. We had little kids running everywhere, screeching and having a great time. Some even brought their dogs. I was in shock at all of the unforeseen things we had to cope with.

One night I heard what sounded like coughing in our bedroom. It went on and on. After realizing it was not Heather, I discovered some of the construction workers were sleeping on the ground just outside the bedroom wall. In fact, the property was so crowded that several of these fellows slept just outside our window, Others tried to sneak into the sanctuary at night and sleep on the padded pews in their dirty work clothes. Every day it seemed there was something really strange or frightening happening that kept me off-kilter. How much longer could I stand the pressure, I wondered?

At night most of the coconuts gradually disappeared from the trees around the church. It was amazing to watch a young Filipino man shimmy up the trunk of a tall palm tree in his bare feet, hack off a coconut with one swipe of his deadly bolo, shove the knife back in his belt, and slide back down in less than a minute. We didn't begrudge the workers helping themselves to a free midnight snack, but a more serious situation was also occurring at night. Apparently, steel rebar (rods) were being stolen, possibly by workmen or their friends, and some of the cement was gradually disappearing.

The only safe place for the steel rebar seemed to be on the tin roof of our parsonage next door. So, all of the rebar was hauled up onto our roof every night. At sunrise as the men started dragging these large steel rods across our metal roof, I cannot tell you how nerve-racking the constant clanging was to the two of us.

Finally, I reached my wits end! The climax came when a huge structural steel beam was about to be delivered. It would connect one side of the building to the other. The problem was, the steel beam must fit exactly together with the rods already in place on the top of the wall. If they did not fit together within a fraction of an inch, there was a chance the entire wall would crumble and the beam would then be unusable. Had I hired the best structural steel engineer, I wondered? Was this man really capable of doing a job that required such precision? Finally, I told Heather, "I cannot take another day of this pressure."

I walked outside as evening approached. The men and their families seemed to have a system in place to fix their meals on the site over little fires. I watched the wispy curls of smoke rising into the air amid the bustle of children and dogs barking. Somehow, I *had* to get away! There were no courses in the seminary that taught how to deal with all this.

Note to the Reader: The events in these stories occurred in the 1980's, over 40 years ago. The Philippine Islands have made tremendous progress in industry and standard of living since those days.

23

Friends of Elvis: The Blackwood Brothers

Our world today is constantly changing. Our own lives and even friendships constantly change through marriage, children, jobs, health issues, friends moving away, and so on. There is one friend who never changes: Jesus Christ. He will never leave nor forsake us. However, we also crave earthly friendships - people who will stick by us throughout our many shifting circumstances.

Interestingly, **Elvis Presley** as a teenager often hung around the concert halls where my friends **Cecil Blackwood** and the **Blackwood Brothers Quartet** were performing. They sometimes gave him a free ticket. After all he was just a poor youth who loved their style and whose name they did not even know. After the concerts, Elvis often meandered around the dressing rooms, fascinated by the music and just wanting to talk with my friends.

About that time Elvis began to ride the church bus to our services at Memphis First Assembly of God, where he joined my Sunday school class. My dad and I sometimes took groceries to the projects where Elvis lived with his parents. His dad was an unemployed truck driver and the family was having a rough time. Later, Elvis rose to a position of world-wide fame, and I saw less of him.

Although we did not communicate often, I had many years of connection with Elvis, but he remained in closer touch with the Blackwood family. This quartet was one of the most popular gospel singing groups at that time. Cecil Blackwood and I had been friends since our teenage days.

Many years later, when we became missionaries to the Philippines, we were delighted when Cecil Blackwood offered to bring the entire quartet plus a tour group, to the Philippines.

We arranged for them to put on concerts in Manila and Clark Air Force Base. Cecil had also promised that when he came, he'd bring our church a state-of-the-art audio system. The whole proposal was so amazing that we wondered if he could make it all come about.

Cecil Blackwood did come as promised and brought with him a tour group and a full audio system. In order to convince the Philippine Customs Department not to charge any duty on it, I had to push my way into the off-limits customs hall and sort of bully my way into where officers were examining Cecil's luggage and the audio system. I introduced myself to the chief customs officer as Pastor Burgess. In this Catholic country they had great respect for priests and ministers. I convinced them that the audio system was not for sale, but would be used for Gospel concerts in our church.

Among the places the quartet sang on that trip was the plush Philippine Convention Center in downtown Manila. The rent for the Center was extremely high, but we were able to sell enough tickets to cover the cost. Further, the Blackwoods asked for no honorarium. The huge auditorium was packed for the event, and the crowd was ecstatic with enthusiasm as they sang.

There appeared one minor glitch that evening. The gentleman that helped organize the ticket sales had suggested earlier that it would be a great idea to have a sit-down banquet in the ballroom of the Convention Center after the concert. It would be for the quartet, their tour group, and a core of people who had helped sell tickets. It was a great idea, but I brushed it off as being impractical, and I never agreed to it.

When the concert concluded that evening and we were all about to leave, "Jim," the money manager, asked if we were going to stay for the banquet. What banquet? None of us had the faintest idea there was going to be a full sit-down dinner. Only a small group who heard about it at the last minute attended. Fortunately, there was enough money remaining from ticket sales to cover the dinner. This ticket salesman was the same money manager who had earlier misplaced $5,000 of our church building fund money. However, that is another story told in a previous chapter.

The quartet also sang in our newly completed church facility outside the American airbase. The coming of these friends had a spectacular effect on our congregation and the entire Christian community there. They sang to a packed auditorium, and the military men and their families especially relished the opportunity to hear American artists. What a celebration to mark the opening of our new building!

James Blackwood (known as "Mr. Gospel Music") kept a busy schedule and did not often appear with the quartet. Yet, James came all the way from Memphis to the Philippines, adding vigor and inspiration to the events. We saw our new church filled to capacity. When James Blackwood was on stage, he must have felt the group needed a bit of help, so he asked me to come to the platform and sing with them. I really think the quartet covered up for my inability, but it was fun, and an honor to sing with them.

Later, I organized concerts for the quartet in Taiwan and Hong Kong. They actually paid all my expenses to fly up to Hong Kong to be with them and to be certain all was well-organized for their arrival and concerts there.

A LITTLE HISTORY OF THE BLACKWOODS

The Blackwood family had become close friends with our family since the week they first moved to Memphis. At this time, they were already the best-known gospel singing group in the US. They had become nationally known after appearing on The Arthur Godfrey Show in New York. The baritone, RW Blackwood, had become an excellent pilot, having flown the quartet's plane 500 hours already. He had flown the group to New York for their appearances on The Arthur Godfrey Show. This was the pinnacle of success for them.

Unfortunately, three weeks later on June 30, 1954, there was a tragic fiery plane crash on an improvised air strip in Clanton, Alabama. The pilot, RW Blackwood, and his copilot, Bill Lyles, were killed instantly. This really hit home to me because as a young teenager RW's son, Ron Blackwood, was my closest friend, and his dad, RW, was my "idol."

Of course, these men, being in their early 40's, had no thought of preplanning any funerals for themselves. They were too young to die. In the crash that shook our region, there was no family member calm enough to make serious funeral decisions. The remaining quartet members and their families asked my dad, Doyle Burgess, to select the caskets, cemetery plots, etc. Fortunately, they had their own funds to cover the expenses. Experiences like these bonded our families together as the years passed. I am sure the quartet would never would have made two trips to join me for concerts in Manila if bonds had not been strengthened over those many years. In these days of such fragile relationships, it has never been more important to build strong friendships founded on love and mutual respect!

The quartet was so devastated by the plane crash that they considered quitting their singing ministry. However, they had a large concert already scheduled in Dallas, Texas for a few days later. James Blackwood said if they cancelled that date, it might be the end of their singing ministry. The Statesmen Quartet of Atlanta, Georgia joined the remaining Blackwoods in Dallas. Two of their members filled in for RW and Bill at the concert that evening. As remaining quartet members recovered somewhat from the tragedy, they asked well-known song writer and base singer, JD Sumner, to join the group. Then James' nephew, Cecil Blackwood, joined completing the team. The quartet continued traveling and inspiring great crowds for many more years.

Meanwhile, over the years **Elvis** had risen from poverty and obscurity to become world famous. Those early contacts with the Blackwood family began a friendship that lasted through the years of Elvis' fame and fortune. One of his body guards stated that in his off hours Elvis only listened to Gospel music. His two favorite groups were the Blackwoods and the Statesmen. As a matter of fact, later on two of the Blackwood group joined Elvis in Vegas for several years. They backed him up when he sang Gospel songs. At Elvis' funeral, his father, Vernon Presley, asked James Blackwood to sing one of Elvis' most favorite songs, "How Great Thou Art." Terry Blackwood, who had sung with Elvis in Vegas, was asked to be a pall bearer.

Today, in the rush of our lives, we often do not realize how critical it is to invest in people. The friendships we nurture will form bonds with folks who will stand with us through all our changing circumstances in life. Also, we should always remember there is one friend who never changes: Jesus. We desperately need His unwavering presence as the one true anchor in our lives.

24

Air Force Chaplain Sent to Leavenworth Federal Prison

SAVED BY A CASKET

Chaplain Tom* was not your ordinary military chaplain. He was always laughing and playing practical jokes. One Sunday morning he actually brought an aluminum casket down the center aisle in our main worship service. We knew Major Tom was different, but we had never seen anything like this! The chaplain explained that our old life was like being in a coffin, but when we ask Jesus to be Lord of our lives, He sets us free to live a new life. He explained we are now dead to sin and a fresh beginning unfolds ahead of us. Many men were touched by that sermon.

About this time, we were planning a service to baptize new believers in our lovely new sanctuary. The night before, we had filled the baptistry with water in preparation for the celebration. I arrived early that Sunday morning just to be sure everything was set. Unfortunately, as I walked across the carpet I noticed an odd sound - squish, squish - with every step! I was stunned to see our beautiful new carpet was soaking wet! The carpet was drenched all the way from the platform to the entrance of the building! I was shocked.

---

* Tom was not his real name.

I am sure you couldn't imagine what the problem was, and neither could I at that moment. No, the baptistry had not overflowed; something worse had happened. I'll tell you what we discovered in a moment.

Unfortunately, even before construction started on this beautiful fan-shaped auditorium, problems began to surface. Of course, we had followed clear specific blueprints as the building was being constructed. However, Heather's dad, being an architect, had warned us that inexperienced contractors often try to cut corners even on small projects like a church baptistry.

Back in the States we would have installed a prefabricated fiberglass container for the water, but these were unavailable in the Philippines. I wanted to be sure our baptistry was done right, although at the time I had no awareness of any potential problems. One thing I advised our contractor to do was to put heavy coatings of waterproofing on the interior of the cement baptistry walls. We had made a special trip into Manila to get waterproofing that was the finest on the market. I explained to the workmen that as soon as the cement on the baptistry interior was dry a heavy coat of waterproofing had to be applied to the cement walls. We were briefly out of town during the final phase of the work and had left the contractor to oversee the baptistry completion.

By now you may have guessed what the problem was. The morning of our first baptismal service, the water in the tank had not overflowed; the problem was the waterproofing had not been applied to the inside walls of the reservoir or possibly had been applied incorrectly. Neither the contractor nor the workmen would tell us what had gone wrong. It is possible the waterproofing was stolen by one of the workmen who had then sold it, or the waterproofing had simply never been applied. But the bottom line was we had a faulty baptistry. So, when it was filled with water the water pressure had pushed through the porous cement blocks that formed the tank and thus had seeped out across the platform floor and down through the entire sanctuary. There was nothing we could do at that late date to fix the problem. I was shaking at the horror of what I was seeing. Our expensive new carpet would probably have to be replaced and the baptism service would have to be postponed. I was literally ill.

But wait! Just maybe there *was* a solution! I suddenly thought about the chaplain's aluminum casket! I made an emergency call to Chaplain Tom on the base and asked him if the coffin was still empty and available. If so, could he lend it to us for that morning's event?

The chaplain was thrilled to comply and immediately had it sent over. We drained what little water was left in the tank, set the coffin in its place, and filled it. The service began. What a service that was! New Christians mostly in their 20's along with a few teens and children testified with deep emotion how God had changed their lives. People clapped and cried and the whole auditorium erupted in praise as each candidate stepped forward to be baptized.

Actually, the aluminum coffin proved to be so effective after that first use, we decided not to try to recoat the baptistry's interior walls. The casket ended up as a permanent fixture, a symbol of the resurrected life in Christ. And, thankfully the carpet dried in a few days with no major damage.

A CASE AGAINST CHAPLAIN TOM

Chaplain Tom was a wonderful committed Christian and also a dear friend of mine and many others in our church family. Just down the road from our church another smaller Christian servicemen's center had been started by some enthusiastic young airmen. This small group was even more tightknit than ours. Chaplain Tom got involved in ministering to them as well. Our men had a good relationship with them and we sometimes got together for special events.

In that smaller center, men often dropped by for snacks and to hang out. And many came to know Jesus as their Savior under Chaplain Tom's ministry there. Unfortunately, most of the fellows never seemed able to locate the offering/donation box as they munched on the snacks. Like many young believers, they seemed to assume that it was someone else's job to pay the food and power bills.

A few of their men did give offerings, but they never came close to tithing and paying all the expenses. Chaplain Tom would often dig into his own pocket and buy groceries and supplies from the air base to take to this new struggling outreach. *But the devil is not happy for people to love and minister together in harmony*. The enemy soon began to cause division in their center.

I never understood what caused all the problems that began to trouble that ministry. They seemed to have something to do with Chaplain Tom's involvement. Tom had been a great friend to their director and all the men who attended that ministry. There must have been a small nucleus that were jealous or just plain bitter about something. *It only takes a dedicated minority to destroy something good!*

Apparently, this so-called dedicated minority found time to search through a thick Air Force regulation book looking for some obscure rule they could use against the chaplain. A small group of local Filipinos had become a part of the group and periodically ate meals with them. The troublemakers found a regulation stating that food from the base could only be used by the American military personnel. So, this small group of antagonizers claimed that the chaplain was not following the letter of the law. They went straight to the base commander to accuse their Christian brother.

If this had been the only accusation against him, it might have been ignored. However, a much bigger issue soon surfaced. The US military had a contract with a shipping company that allowed it to ship one vehicle per family back to the USA for free. As an additional bonus, the Philippine government allowed that same vehicle to be shipped out of the country tax free. Tom wanted to ship home two vehicles rather than just the one he owned.

Tom was fascinated with the skill of the local Filipino mechanics and sheet metal workers. These men could take the frame of almost any kind of car, even one that had been heavily damaged, and with a few weeks of work make it look similar to any type of vehicle a person could want. These local craftsmen customized vehicles to closely resemble Thunderbirds, Mercedes, etc. The end results may not always have been perfect, but they always looked very impressive. Unfortunately, the biggest problem customers had with these remade vehicles usually involved the wiring. Sometimes they wouldn't start!

Chaplain Tom saw the chance to make easy money by transporting one of these autos back home for himself and a second one to sell. The trouble was, he was only allowed to send one vehicle home when he returned to the States. He found an airman who did not plan to ship a vehicle back to the USA, and who was willing to ship Tom's second vehicle by claiming it was his own. In turn the shipping and tax on it would be free. Obviously, this was dishonest.

In time, the news of Tom's deception leaked out. This was a major crime that would soon cost him much trouble. The base commander was irate when he learned what the chaplain had planned to do. Tom was not only severely reprimanded, but action was taken to put him on trial in a military court martial. This is the most serious thing that can happen to anybody in our armed forces.

When the chaplain found out he was actually going to be accused of fraud and theft of government property, he was shaken. However, the military offered to provide him a defense lawyer who was supposed to be excellent, at no cost to him. Chaplain Tom refused the offer and decided to send to the States to get a civilian lawyer. When the officers who were reviewing Tom's case found out he was bringing in an outsider for his defense they were upset. That was a breach of protocol and an insult to them.

As the investigation continued, Tom seemed nonchalant and somewhat arrogant about it. He knew that the military had never sent a chaplain to prison before, and he did not expect to be the first. Since by this time his wrong-doing was widely known, his cocky attitude did not sit well with the base authorities.

When the court martial began, I sat in on all the trial proceedings. The lawyer Tom had hired seemed somewhat detached or indifferent. When it came time for him to defend Tom, he had very little to say. During a break I pled with Tom, "Please, you hired this man at high cost to you. You paid his airfare from the U.S. to the Philippines, his hotel bill, plus his legal fees. He *must* speak strongly in your defense!"

But Tom remained unconcerned. "The military," he said, "would never send a chaplain to prison." When the verdict came down, Tom was found guilty of all the charges against him. He lost his new rank as Major, was heavily fined, and sentenced to a stiff term at Leavenworth Federal Prison. He was in shock. This was not supposed to happen, but it did.

Now Tom simply had to wait for all the paperwork to be finished so he could be released and sent on a special flight out of Clark Airbase to the States. Until then he was allowed to stay in the area. He attended services regularly at our church and we often had him in our home for meals. Our people who knew all the facts still treated him as a brother who needed encouragement, though they did not excuse what he had done.

Tom had been humiliated, with his arrogance and cocky attitude gone. He was now a convicted felon. What a horrible thing this was, especially since he was supposed to be an example to others of a born-again believer as well as an ordained minister.

It is clear that Tom's major problem was greed - just wanting a little extra money. It cost him severely. He received a heavy fine, a reduction in rank, plus he had to pay his lawyer and all the lawyer's travel expenses from the USA to Manila.

This unfortunate story is a lesson to all of us who seek to bend the law and perhaps get some easy money. Our hearts were broken because of Tom's failure and good example his life could have been to others.

I do not remember the exact details of Tom's being sent to prison. I am not aware of how long his prison sentence was, but I do know that this gave him a heavy dose of humility and that eventually he was released. His dream was to start a new church in his hometown in Texas. I believe he did, and in time regained his self-respect.

25

Escape to the Mountains – Near the Breaking Point

I had totally had it with the building project! Tomorrow, the final steel beam would arrive, and a crane would lift it to the top of the building. The crane would drop it in the specific place prepared for it on top of the walls, thus joining both sides of the building together. I was not convinced that the fittings to receive the steel beam would end up being perfectly aligned, nor was I sure that the walls would stand the stress of this gigantic beam.

The uncertainty of the outcome was the final straw. I confessed to Heather that I had reached the point where I totally surrendered the matter into the Lord's hands. I could do no more. I told Heather that we and the children were leaving town and going a hundred miles north up to the mountains to the cool climate of Baguio City. Heather was a real champ during this entire ordeal. I told her that even if the walls collapse, we would be in Baguio and I did not want anybody to contact me about any building problems. I could carry the load no longer.

We had a refreshing three or four days in the cool mountain air before we headed back down the mountain to the hot humid conditions of Clark Air Base. I approached the church site with some trepidation, knowing that if the walls had totally collapsed, the whole project would be a disaster. That's not what you call positive thinking or positive confession. That was just a mental state I had reached. When we drove up to the front of the church I was amazed and tears trickled down my cheeks. Everything was completed just like it was supposed to! The building was magnificent!

I made a promise to the church, probably unwisely, that I would not leave the Philippines until all of our loans were arranged to be paid in full. The time had come for our furlough and for Deborah and Som to be enrolled in school in Memphis. It was a lonely day when I took Heather, Deborah, and Som to the Manila airport to board their flight for Memphis. **I did not have the faintest idea when I would be able to join them again**.

I asked Heather to do some things that were way beyond her comfort zone. At this point, all of our funds had been expended. And then I remembered a Christian allergist in Memphis who had made an unusual offer. I knew some of his partners, but did not know him well at all. Earlier he had volunteered, "If you ever need financial help, let me know." I knew Heather was very reluctant to talk to anybody about money, but it looked certain that unless we made some unusual arrangements, I was going to be living in the Philippine church parsonage indefinitely. So, when Heather arrived in Memphis, she went to see the allergist and told him about our building project. At my direction, she asked if we could borrow $1,000 for three months. He reached into his desk drawer and brought out his checkbook. **He wrote a check for not $1,000, but a check for $3,000! She was aghast and told him we probably could never repay this huge sum. The doctor said, "This is not a loan, but a gift!"**

Also, while Heather was in Memphis, a cousin lent us money which we later repaid. Now we had done everything conceivable and it was time to rest in the Lord's hands. Other funds came in. One little Filipina lady had saved all of her money and purchased a 22-karat gold necklace. It was quite common in Asia for people to put their savings into gold jewelry. When this young lady who worked as a house maid saw the need of the church building, she brought her gold necklace and laid it on the altar. It would have been the equivalent of 2 years wages for her. Many others made sacrificial gifts. Finally, all of the outstanding debts had been paid and I bought my plane ticket for Memphis.

My two best buddies, Lloyd Francis and John Burkinbine, drove me the 70 miles to the Manila airport. I felt we had arranged for the finest missionary couple to fill in for us while we were on furlough. As we traveled toward the airport, I said to John and Lloyd, "The couple that are replacing us are first class. I only wish I could've met them."

John and Lloyd stared at each other in disbelief. Finally, they said, "The replacements have been in the house with you for nearly 3 weeks, ate all their meals with you, and you had countless conversations with them. **Are you trying to say that you have no recollection of ever seeing them?" I shook my head, knowing that it was well past time for me to have a break!**

I took one last look at the beautiful new sanctuary, now completed and paid for, standing in a prominent place outside Clark Air Force Base, welcoming all to come and worship. **We had VENTURED WHERE FEW WOULD HAVE WANTED OR DARED TO GO! But God had led us at every step. The end result was worth everything.**

Meet The Author

DEEP IN DEBT AND NO WAY TO REPAY

I owe a debt so great I can never repay it. The greatest debt that any of us owes is to Jesus for giving his life for us on Calvary! Also, I'm grateful that down through the years there have been countless numbers of people who have had input into my life. Someone has said, "You become a part of every person you meet, and they become a part of you!"

Those people that surround us have the greatest influence on our lives. Unfortunately, there are a host of people who have been surrounded by folks who dragged them down rather than lifted them up.

I am very blessed that many people in my life have believed in me, prayed for me, and encouraged me, especially in my early days of public ministry.

Willard Cantelon is one man who took a personal interest in me and my future ministry. Rev Cantelon was a tall, red-haired Canadian evangelist. His ministry had carried him to a great many countries of the world. I was fascinated that this brilliant man could quote large volumes of scripture from memory and he never used any sermon notes. Not only was he an interesting speaker, but he had a great command of world events and history.

He was also an artist. Each evening at church, he would use oil paints to depict scenes of his travels, especially in some of the mountains in Europe. After 15 minutes of painting, accompanied by music, he would award these paintings to those who brought the most guests. After church, he always seemed to find time to chat with me. I was enthralled by the stories of his travel and ministry.

In my early 20's I was at a crossroads. I was a pharmacy school student and lay preacher. Periodically I had debated about full-time ministry. But wisdom seemed to dictate that I should follow my father in his pharmacy business. I always enjoyed preaching where there were open doors in area churches. I was deeply involved as a layman because I realized not everyone who was a committed Christian was called to be a full-time minister. However, I had always wondered what it would be like to visit some of these missionaries like Brother Cantelon who had come to our church, and see their ministries in other countries.

At that time, my dad owned 3 pharmacies in Memphis. He challenged me with this proposal: if I could graduate from University of Tennessee College of Pharmacy and then pass the rigorous State Pharmacy Board exams, he would send me on a 2-week trip to Europe.

In those years, I really enjoyed preaching in local churches on the week-ends more than counting pills in the pharmacy. Other doors began to open for ministry. I was invited to direct a weekly TV program at 6:45 AM on Fridays from the famous Peabody Hotel. For my TV appearance, I got unusual pay – a free breakfast at the luxurious Peabody coffee shop. Unfortunately, that didn't put gas in my tank. The program was called "Above the Clouds," started by Jimmy Stroud, who also pioneered Memphis Union Mission. It aired on the best-known network, and was viewed all over the mid-south. Back then, being on TV weekly, greatly helped me become acquainted in the region.

Besides TV, I was part of a brand-new national ministry to troubled youth called "Lifeline," also under Jimmy Stroud's leadership. Through Lifeline I initiated a regular ministry at the Memphis Juvenile Court for teenage boys as well as girls. One year I was brave enough to organize a summer youth camp for boys. Many of these boys had never been outside their troubled neighborhoods. We only had one escapee during that week, but the local sheriff quickly found him.

One night during evangelist Cantelon's ministry in our church in Memphis, I told him a bit about myself and my limited ministry background. Then I mentioned that my father had offered to send me to Europe for 2 weeks. Hesitantly I told him that I thought it would be fantastic if I could speak in some of the churches in Europe. But who was I as a 23-year-old, and now a pharmacy graduate, to fill pulpits in major cities in Europe? I expected he would be shocked at the suggestion and change the subject. However, to my amazement he offered to help me organize an itinerary that would take me through the major capitals of Europe. I was speechless. He was sticking his neck out for me as a kid, to speak in churches throughout the continent, beginning in London, through a number of capitals in Europe and all the way to Jerusalem.

Obviously, this kind of schedule would take a whole lot more than 2 weeks. Thus, I approached my dad and asked him to loan me enough money to stay for 3 months to preach in the churches in Europe and visit our missionaries. Graciously, he agreed.(Yes, I did repay him later.)

Rev. Cantelon suggested that I travel through Toronto, Canada, where I would then go on to board a ship in Montreal, headed for Europe. He helped arrange a service for me in a large church in Toronto.

The visit to Toronto would forever change my life! But a last-minute change of plans re-routed me to speak at Danforth Gospel Temple in Toronto, rather than the church at which I had planned to be. That Sunday night during the service, I noticed a very attractive young lady sitting down front. I got up enough courage to speak to her mother after church, and found this young lady's name was Heather Reed. Mrs. Reed graciously invited me to come to their home for a snack. This visit to their home began a 2-year mail box romance between Heather and me. All through my journey to Europe I would send her picture post cards from the cities I visited. On my return home, thanks to the telephone and the mail man, our connections deepened.

Now, ahead of me lay 3 months of traveling alone in Europe. There would be gigantic train depots where little English was spoken, and I would need to find hotel rooms in strange cities, edible food, and stay on budget.

The services in Europe went very well, but I realized that I was "in way over my head." Again, at just 23 years of age I was meeting outstanding pastors, speaking to large congregations, and yes, I was still only a kid. My life was totally altered by this 3-month adventure. Finally, I began to understand that God had a plan for me in the full-time ministry beyond counting pills in a pharmacy. That realization did not give me a feeling of arrogance, but of humility. I felt unworthy of such opportunities at such a young age. I owed a debt to the many people who believed in me and opened doors for me in those early years.

A QUICK TRANSITION

Heather Anne Reed Becomes "Sister Burgess"

An Accidental Meeting

The likelihood of my meeting Heather after church that Sunday night, was extremely remote. I stopped in Toronto enroute to board the ship in Montreal for Europe. My friend, Willard Cantelon had booked me to speak in one of the largest churches in Toronto. Due to a last-minute change in their plans, I ended up at Danforth Gospel Tabernacle, a much smaller church. As I spoke there that Sunday night, I noticed a very attractive young lady sitting close to the front. I desperately wanted to find out who she was. (Young ladies, if you'd like to catch the eye of a visiting single guest speaker, sit down front.) When church was over, I approached a lady I presumed to be Heather's mother, and risked asking her, "Where do the young people meet after church on Sunday nights?"

She replied she did not know what the young people were doing, but I was welcome to come to their house for a snack when the service was over. Thus, I ended up at Heather's home and got acquainted with her parents, Frank and Lillian Reed. The following day, her brother Bryan took me all around the vast city of Toronto, population 1 million back then. That evening I had a lovely supper with their family, and of course, I got Heather's address. During my journeys through Europe, I kept in touch with her through picture post cards from various cities where I was speaking.

Once back in Memphis, I took a research assistant position at University of Tennessee and was busy in various scientific projects. One project involved searching for some useful benefit from the hallucinogenic molecule, LSD.

As spring of 1963 approached, Heather's parents were considering a trip from Toronto down to Tuscaloosa, Alabama to visit relatives. I'm sure the Reeds wondered about this guy from Memphis that seemed to have so many stories. I think they noticed that there was some kind of a spark in my relationship with their daughter, even though we had only spoken twice, and that was 9 months ago. The Reed family detoured by Memphis for 2 or 3 days on the way to Alabama. My folks invited Heather to stay in our guest room, so at last we could talk face to face, as her brother and parents continued on to Alabama.

Our First Date - A Trip to the Jail!

Heather and I were just chatting on the back porch that first evening, when my dad stuck his head out the door and ordered, "Gene, you need to go down to the jail and get your Uncle Jack out." This was our first official date - a trip to the jail. I wanted to make a great impression on her, but I sure hadn't thought of a late-night trip to downtown Memphis. My Uncle Jack was partly sober by the time we picked him up, so Heather and I drove him across town to his irate wife. This kind of event would have scared the average girl away.

Fortunately, Heather stuck with our friendship through a variety of other bizarre Southern cultural experiences. In the daytime during Heather's visit, I had to leave her for my teaching assignments down at UT. Also, in the 1960's, racial conflicts had begun to cause unrest in many cities, and Memphis was no exception. Heather had several friends of various ethnicities at the University of Toronto, and was bewildered by the many racial conflicts she saw in the South such as sit-in's etc. Added to those disenchantments, my youngest brother Phillip woke her up the first morning after her arrival and asked her to make him some breakfast. She was stunned. She, a guest, was being asked to make the host breakfast? As I remember, she giggled, told him to make his own breakfast, and went back to bed. Events like this, happening in a single week, would have destroyed most relationships. Thank God that although Heather was shocked, she stuck with me.

Time flew by. Heather returned to Toronto, but she came back to Memphis that summer. At this time, I was at a crossroads, thinking more seriously about full-time ministry. I had spoken at a number of churches in the Mid-South, but to my bewilderment, many people thought I was from a wealthy family and did not need much of an offering. I soon realized that if I was going to survive financially, I had to get out of the Mid-South. That is when a rare opportunity opened up. A teen-age girls' trio from our church had been invited to sing at a huge Youth Camp in Pennsylvania. Word came to me that if I went with them as a camp counselor, I might be invited to speak in area churches on Sundays. This seemed like a golden opportunity to "spread my wings." But there was a "minor" problem: Heather had come 1000 miles on a Greyhound bus from Toronto to visit me for the summer. Now I was debating about leaving her with friends in Memphis for 2 weeks. I was conflicted. It would be a terrible insult to leave Heather alone for 2 weeks while I hung out with 3 teen-age girls and their chaperone in Pennsylvania. How could I tell Heather of my plans? Yet the possibility of new open doors for ministry was intriguing. With Heather's reluctant approval, I made the choice to go, and as it turned out, many doors did open for future ministry in the Eastern States.

Heather returned to Toronto to complete her BA degree, but not before agreeing to become my wife after graduating. I was elated! As for me, the ministry became a more compelling career than pharmacy, and I made the decision to make it my life's vocation. As our wedding grew closer, the only request I made for the ceremony was that my dear friend, Ken Carter would sing, *"Whither Thou Goest, I Will Go."* Ken and Sherry came all the way from Washington, DC to sing at the wedding. And since then, Heather has followed me through jungles and deserts. She has slept in palaces and shacks, through stifling heat and arctic cold. She has been a mother to our children. Wherever I felt God leading me, she has been at my side, presenting puppet stories and rallies for the children as I preached to teens and adults, so that our meetings embraced the whole family.

She sees the beauty and humor in the most difficult situations. On one occasion, in a remote island in the Philippines, we stayed in a bamboo house up on stilts. Under the house, pigs grunted as they routed around looking for a snack. I desperately wanted a cold coke, but there were no refrigerators on the island. I was trying to get comfortable that night, lying on a hard plywood "mattress," when a chicken flew through the bedroom window. I started to complain to Heather about the accommodations, when she sighed and said, "Isn't this romantic? Look at that yellow moon peeking through the palm leaves of the roof. It's shining on the white sand on the beach, and making a path across the water. It's so beautiful."

I constantly thank God for the "coincidences" that put us together, and His constant blessing that has made our lives full and beautiful.

In one short ceremony, Heather went from being Miss Reed, to "Sister Burgess," a name she loathed, but which was a common term used in the South when referring to a pastor's wife. She has been a *sister* to many women, and a faithful loving companion to me. I thank God for this soulmate, counselor, friend, encourager and much more, that He has blessed me with during these past 56 years of marriage.

Printed in the United States
by Baker & Taylor Publisher Services